TASTES & TREASURES

A Storytelling Cookbook of Historic Arizona

HISTORICAL LEAGUE, INC.

TASTES & TREASURES
A Storytelling Cookbook of Historic Arizona

Published by Historical League, Inc.

Copyright © 2007 by
Historical League, Inc.
1300 North College Avenue
Tempe, Arizona 85281
480-929-0292
www.historicalleague.com
Photographs © by Werner Seggara

This cookbook is a collection of favorite recipes, which are not necessarily original recipes.

Library of Congress Control Number: 2006924349
ISBN-10: 0-9768363-0-0
ISBN-13: 978-0-97683-630-8

Edited, Designed and Manufactured by
Favorite Recipes® Press
An imprint of

FRP™

P. O. Box 305142
Nashville, Tennessee 37230
800-358-0560

Art Director: Steve Newman
Book Design: Brad Whitfield and Susan Breining
Project Editor: Linda A. Jones

Manufactured in the United States of America
First Printing: 2007
10,000 copies
Second Printing: 2008
10,000 copies

Acknowledgments

It is a pleasure to acknowledge the companies and individuals whose generosity made this book possible.

ARIZONA

HISTORICAL

Wells Fargo Bank, N.A.

SOCIETY

Ruth and Al McLeod, in memory of her parents,
Mildred and Ron Oake

LEAGUE

Tom Chauncey, Linda Corderman, Gaye Ingram, Zona Lorig, Gail and Charles Lucky,
Susan Oelze, Donna Jensen Roe, Terrie Sanford, Patsy Tait

FRIEND

Linda and Sam Cathey, Nancy Evans, Ruth Ann and Phil Hogan, Kay and Rex Holcombe,
Dianne Linthicum, Jeannine and Jim Moyle, Peggy Murphy, Mary and Bill Parker,
Pam Knight Stevenson, Mary and Rob Ward

ANGEL

Rowene Aguirre-Medina, Leslie and John Christiansen, Pat and Peter Faur, Linda Fritsch,
Rose Mofford, Emma Lou Bennett Philabaum

Early Arizona Hospitality

ROUGH, RAGGED AND NOT FOR SISSIES

Arizona's wonderful reputation today as a place of elegant hotels, restaurants and great cuisine had rough and humble beginnings. Lieutenant John G. Bourke arrived in the territory with the army in 1870 and would later write about a visit to Tucson that same year in which he described visiting the famous Shoo Fly Restaurant.

"It was a long, narrow, low ceiled room of adobe, whose walls were washed in a neutral yellowish tint, whose floor was rammed earth and ceiling of white muslin."

The restaurant had pinewood tables and homemade chairs with rawhide seats. On duty were two bright, pleasant-mannered Mexican boys wearing neat white cotton jackets and loose white cotton trousers, with a colored sash about the waist. Each was armed with a flyswatter as a badge of office—something that, no doubt, provided the inspiration for the restaurant's name.

Meals consisted mostly of bacon, chicken and mutton. There was plenty of jerked beef, palatable in stews and the ubiquitous "frijoles," or beans. Potatoes were a luxury and "fresh fruit" was hauled by burro train all the way from Hermosillo, Sonora.

The territorial capital of Prescott got into the hospitality business at a place called Fort Misery, a log cabin that was the town's first building. It was built by Manual Ysario, who soon abandoned it, and a lady named Caroline Ramos moved in and turned it into a boardinghouse. Ms. Ramos was known as "Virgin Mary" because of her generosity in helping the sick and injured miners. The menu offered few choices: breakfast, lunch and dinner consisting of venison, chiles, goat's milk, tortillas and coffee. Room and board was $25 a week in gold—in advance.

Fort Misery was also used as a church on Sunday, and during the week Judge John "Blinky" Howard dispensed justice or "misery" as the raucous residents called it. And that's how the establishment got its name.

Another place of hospitality for weary travelers was located in the thick pine forest along the old Crook Military Road between Fort Apache and Fort Verde. Walter Rigney, a tall man with bushy hair and known as "Old Pinetop," was the host.

Stagecoach travel in early Arizona wasn't for sissies. Passengers were appalled by the dirt and squalor that greeted them at the stations. The interiors were black with flies. They were built of adobe with floors that were, as one traveler wrote, "much like the ground outside, but not as clean." Meals were worse, serving tough beef or fried pork, coarse bread, mesquite beans, lethally black coffee and often a mysterious concoction known as "slumgullion."

The frontier eventually drew to a close in the late 1800s, and during the early years of the twentieth century Americans became more mobile. Passenger trains and "horseless carriages" now carried tourists in relative comfort into places heretofore visited only by the most adventuresome. The new breed demanded better facilities and food. An Englishman named Fred Harvey set the standard with his hotels and fine restaurants located along the Santa Fe Railroad line.

Among those was the famous Harvey House in my hometown of Ash Fork. The Escalante was mission-style Spanish architecture. Built in 1897, it was billed as "one of the most important of the string of beautiful Harvey Houses on the Santa Fe," and said to be the best hotel west of Chicago. Fabled "Route 66" curved around behind the hotel.

The Escalante had a newsstand where customers could get the latest edition of eastern newspapers, a curio shop where one could purchase Indian arts and crafts, a barber shop, a saloon and an elegant restaurant where customers were served by the storied Harvey Girls. Like so many others, it's gone now but those vintage establishments that remain are time-honored reminders of our past.

MARSHALL TRIMBLE
Official Arizona State Historian

Let's Make History

In the beginning... The Arizona Historical Society is Arizona's oldest historical, cultural organization and was established by an Act of the First Territorial Legislature in Prescott on November 7, 1864. It is noteworthy that one of the earliest actions by those engaged in creating a new territorial government was to authorize the means for documenting the past and recording contemporary events as they unfolded. These architects of the Territory's code of laws realized they were making history and it was important to preserve a record of their actions. Consequently, an organization charged with collecting and preserving "all facts relating to the history of this Territory" engendered a sense of place and defined an identity of those who participated in Arizona's formative years.

These fledgling steps toward preserving territorial history were followed by formal, lively meetings at the Congress Hall Saloon and Palace Hotel in Tucson, where saloonkeepers, merchants, ranchers, freighters and other leading citizens hammered out the governing structure of what was then known as the Society of Arizona Pioneers. Without documentation, we presume those august gentlemen of the Arizona frontier enjoyed ample meals, a variety of libations, cigars and other forms of tobacco requiring spittoons.

From the early 1880s, Society members collected all manner of books, maps, papers and objects reflecting the spirit of their times to enlighten future generations. Following statehood in 1912, the new legislature acknowledged the importance of the Society, re-established it as a trustee agency of Arizona and appropriated modest funding to support its work. Today, statewide holdings in the four AHS museums number more than three million objects.

And, today... Arizona's extraordinarily rich history reflects Native American cultures, the impact of Spanish and Mexican exploration and colonization, America's expansion and the rugged individuals who homesteaded the West, along with recent development and urbanization. Blessed with many stories to tell, the irreplaceable collections give life to Arizona stories. From Wyatt Earp's pistol and Geronimo's medicine bag, to the Empress Carlota's jewels, a child's doll and a pioneer woman's quilt, to taped interviews with Barry Goldwater and John F. Long, or a video of an early Wallace and Ladmo show, the Arizona Historical Society preserves Arizona history for all.

Anne Woosley

ANNE I. WOOSLEY, PH.D.
Executive Director, Arizona Historical Society

Welcome to Arizona Historical Society Museum at Papago Park

The Arizona Historical Society Museum at Papago Park complements the delights that await you in **Tastes & Treasures—A Storytelling Cookbook of Historic Arizona**. *Both offer a savory blend of past and future and of stories and substance, steeped in the richness of Arizona history. The recipes on the pages ahead, like historical documents, are waiting to be realized and reinterpreted today—and tomorrow—in our kitchens and on our palates. In the same way, the unique experiences that have made Arizona what it is today are brought to life in the museum's exhibitions and educational programs.*

As the Central Division of the Arizona Historical Society, the Museum at Papago Park fulfills a pivotal role in establishing a sense of place and purpose for all Arizonans. Our job is to make a place that invites conversations about Arizona's future based on what we know about its past. We have wonderful ingredients to use for creating compelling and inviting spaces that open doors to conversation. Objects evoke one story after another, photographs and oral histories bridge time, and creative people— staff and volunteers alike—make your experience vivid and personal. We would love to share this experience with you.

We depend on generosity to achieve our goals. The energetic involvement of Historical League members in so many areas of our museum keeps us moving forward. As volunteers working with the public, with staff, and with projects such as **Tastes & Treasures**, *Historical League members are the lifeblood of our institution. We are continually conscious of, and always grateful for, their innumerable contributions.*

PETER WELSH, PH.D.
Director
Arizona Historical Society Museum at Papago Park

Meet the Historical League

The Historical League, Inc., supports the educational effort of the Arizona Historical Society Museum at Papago Park in Tempe, Arizona. Organized in 1979, the League also raises money through the combined volunteer efforts of its members.

"Old Ned," an antique toy horse on display at the museum, is the League's logo. The poignant story of a little boy who owned this toy touched the hearts of the founding League members. He died very young but not before handing the toy to his mother, saying, "Take good care of Old Ned."

Members enjoy regular tours of Arizona's historical locations, buildings and other museums. These well-planned adventures embrace friendly and educational interaction among members. An overnight tour is also an exciting segment of the annual tours program.

Special events, under the leadership and direction of members, raise money to provide historical information, maintain archives and library materials, create exhibits and promote the museum. The Children's Holiday Party offers families the opportunity to share a special social occasion, along with personal visits with Mr. and Mrs. Santa Claus. Children are engaged in activities and interactive games before the holiday lunch, while parents, grandparents and other guests shop a well-stocked boutique and bid on special items in the silent auction. There are also toy raffles and entertainment provided by local talent.

The Historymakers Gala, unique to the Historical League, recognizes and honors outstanding Arizonans and also celebrates Arizona's Statehood Day, February 14, 1912. These notable Historymakers contribute to the museum's artifact, oral history and photographic collections. Funds raised by this premier event are used by the museum to build new exhibits and support ongoing programs.

We hope you enjoy using the recipes collected from some of Arizona's treasured, hospitable destinations and reading their stories in TASTES & TREASURES—**A Storytelling Cookbook of Historic Arizona.**

The Historical League is strong because of its members, who volunteer their hearts, time, talent and generosity to preserving the history of Arizona.

About the Book

By the end of 2003, the Historical League's first cookbook, Arizona Cooking Heritage, *had sold out its 6,000-copy print run. A handful of League members met to discuss some ideas for a new cookbook, and it was decided the theme should be a selection of Arizona's historic properties of hospitality.*

An establishment or the building in which a selected site is located must be at least 50 years old. Because the state has a wealth of wonderful hotels, resorts, bed-and-breakfasts and restaurants, it was difficult to adhere to this guideline. And, while the notable chefs contribute much to the cuisine of the Grand Canyon State, because of their transient nature, the focus remains mostly on the establishments.

We also wanted to further recognize the Historical League's Historymakers and include a chapter with their favorite recipes and food-related family memories. Be sure to see "Dolly's Mud Pies," by Historymaker and Family Circus *cartoon artist Bil Keane.*

Excited and interested Historical League members have contributed recipes as well as hours of cooking in test kitchens. See members' delicious recipes in the chapter "Lunch at the Museum."

Contacting the historical sites was educational and rewarding. We are most grateful to establishment owners/managers for their historical notes, and to their chefs for the recipes. We are bringing you the "best of the best."

This book is for everyone, whether you try a new recipe or simply enjoy reading about Arizona's historic hospitality. We wish you a "mouth-watering" good time.

Writers and Editors:
Gaye G. Ingram
Donna Jensen Roe

Table of Contents

Table of Contents

CAMERON TRADING POST

"Discover What We've Spent a Lifetime Learning"

Nearly a century ago in 1911, a suspension bridge was built over the Little Colorado River Gorge. Soon after, in 1916, two brothers, Hubert and C.D. Richardson, established the Cameron Trading Post and filled it with dry goods to barter with Navajo and Hopi locals for wool, blankets and livestock. Those who came to trade were treated well, like family, and they were fed and provided with a place to stay at the trading post.

A trip to Cameron took days of travel by horse-drawn wagon and was often for more than trading and buying goods. The Richardson brothers were trusted by the local Native American people. Because they understood local dialects and customs, they were able to interpret confusing American social customs and legal documents for their customers. The Cameron Trading Post's reputation soon drew other travelers to visit and enjoy their hospitality.

Cameron is located at the east end of the Grand Canyon, north of Flagstaff, on the road to Page. Visitors who may have been "just passing through," on their way to the Canyon, often stay the night in a modern motel room. They are intrigued by today's Indian Lodge where they can shop for Native American Indian Art and dine in the beautiful dining room with its large stone fireplace, tall picture windows and a pressed tin ceiling.

Owners of the Cameron Trading Post today are current employees, many whose roots in the area are generations deep. A descendant of the original founders, the current president maintains the philosophy of hospitality and respect established long ago by the Richardson brothers.

Luncheon Menu

• Navajo Taco

• Navajo Fry Bread

Seasonal Fresh Fruit *or*

Cheesecake with Blueberry Topping

• *Recipes Included*

Cameron Trading Post

Navajo Taco

1¹/2 pounds lean ground beef
1 (8-ounce) can chili sauce
   (for this recipe, Hunt's brand
   was used for testing)
³/4 teaspoon cumin seeds
¹/4 teaspoon dried oregano
¹/2 teaspoon garlic powder
¹/4 teaspoon crushed dried hot
   red chiles
¹/4 teaspoon dried paprika

¹/4 teaspoon salt
1¹/2 pounds cooked pinto beans
8 to 10 pieces of Navajo Fry Bread
   (below)
4 to 5 cups shredded iceberg lettuce
3¹/2 to 4 cups (14 to 16 ounces)
   shredded Cheddar cheese
3 tomatoes, sliced, chopped or
   cut into wedges
1 to 1¹/4 cups chopped green chiles

Brown the ground beef in a skillet, stirring until crumbly; drain. Add the chili sauce, cumin seeds, oregano, garlic powder, hot red chiles, paprika and salt. Simmer for 1 hour, stirring occasionally. Stir in the beans and cook until heated through. To serve, place each piece of fry bread on a large plate and spread each with enough of the chili to almost cover. Layer each with ¹/2 cup lettuce, 6 tablespoons cheese, two tomato slices and 2 tablespoons green chiles. Have big plates and appetites! Nizhoni! (That's Navajo for "beautiful.")

Serves 8 to 10

Navajo Fry Bread

Shortening for deep-frying
7 cups all-purpose flour
1¹/2 teaspoons baking powder

¹/2 teaspoon salt
¹/2 cup milk
¹/2 cup water

Heat the shortening in a deep fryer to 380 to 400 degrees. Mix the flour, baking powder and salt in a bowl. Add the milk and water and mix to form a firm dough. Pinch off a baseball-size piece of the dough and roll or shape by hand to the size of a dinner plate. Deep-fry until the bread is golden brown. Drain on paper towels. Repeat with the remaining dough. Serve hot with honey or confectioners' sugar.

Note: To fry in a skillet, add enough shortening to fill the skillet about 1 inch. Fry the dough in the hot shortening until golden brown, turning after 15 to 20 seconds.

Makes 8 to 10

THE COTTAGE PLACE RESTAURANT
"Best Fine Dining in Flagstaff"

Richard and Edith Bongberg built their bungalow in 1909, a common architectural style
in Flagstaff in the early years of the 20th century. The Bongbergs reared a family
of six children and lived in the home until 1923 when the family moved to California.
Mr. Bongberg, former mayor of Flagstaff, worked at today's Northern Arizona University.

Robert and Mary Riordan (an established historic name in Flagstaff)
bought the home in the 1930s and lived there five years.

A butcher who worked for the Babbitts, Mr. Gamble, was the next owner until
the mid-1950s when he sold to John and Teresa Ortiz, and their family of four children.
"The House on the Corner" became the Tortilla Factory, a thriving family business,
after Teresa began selling her homemade tortillas.

Members of the Bongberg, Riordan, Gamble and Ortiz families frequently
drop by to dine at The Cottage Place, and they love to share their memories
of living there with current owners Frank and Nancy Branham.

The Branhams became owners of record in November 1994. Nancy and Frank,
an award-winning executive chef, have earned their way into the hearts (and stomachs)
of locals and tourists alike. Accolades include "Best Restaurant in Flagstaff,"
Arizona Republic, "Best Fine Dining in Flagstaff," *Arizona Daily Sun*
and ongoing "Awards of Excellence" *Wine Spectator*.

Current customer buzz sings the restaurant's praises: "Dinner was sensual to the
taste buds and the staff was very attentive and caring." Another satisfied diner added:
"Awesome, beyond excellent—it was perfect."

DINNER MENU

- ◆ Seafood Tower
- Salmon Bisque
- ◆ Exotic Greens with Strawberry Vinaigrette
- ◆ Rack of Lamb with Two Sauces
- ◆ Herb-Roasted Vegetables
- ◆ Roasted Red Potatoes
- ◆ Arizona Cream with Raspberry Purée

COCKTAIL PARTY

- Champagne
- ◆ Mojitos
- ◆ Stuffed Mushrooms
- Brie en Croûte
- ◆ Crab Cakes with Corn Sauce
- ◆ Tiropitas

- ◆ *Recipes Included*

The Cottage Place Restaurant

Seafood Tower

1 cup water
1/4 cup Cilantro Lime Vinaigrette (page 21)
1 teaspoon salt
4 large shrimp, peeled and deveined
2 scallops, cleaned
1/4 cup Cilantro Lime Vinaigrette (page 21)
Tomato Caper Relish (page 20)
Horseradish Cream Sauce (page 20)
Bottled cocktail sauce
Avocado fans
Cilantro Lime Vinaigrette (page 21)

Bring the water, 1/4 cup vinaigrette and the salt to a boil in a small saucepan. Add the shrimp and scallops and reduce the heat to 170 degrees. Poach the shrimp and scallops for 5 minutes or until the shrimp turn pink. Remove from the heat. Add ice to the mixture to stop the cooking process and let stand for 4 minutes. Drain the shrimp and scallops and place in a large bowl. Add 1/4 cup vinaigrette and toss to coat. Chill in the refrigerator.

Cut each scallop into three thin circles. Place two plastic tubes 2 inches in diameter and 3 inches tall on a plate. Fill each tube half full with the relish and compact with a spoon handle. Arrange three scallop slices on the relish in each tube. Slide the tip of a metal spatula under each tube and place each on a chilled serving plate. Make a pool of the horseradish cream sauce around the tube. Drag a wooden pick through cocktail sauce and make a design in the horseradish cream sauce. Arrange the poached shrimp and avocado fans in the sauce. Drizzle some of the remaining vinaigrette around the edge of each plate. Remove the plastic tube by pressing down on the scallops with a spoon handle, while lifting each tube.

Serves 2

Tomato Caper Relish

1/2 cup chopped tomato
1/4 cup chopped, seeded peeled cucumbers
1 tablespoon chopped green onion tops
2 teaspoons capers
1/2 teaspoon balsamic vinegar
1/2 teaspoon fresh lemon juice
1/2 teaspoon salt
1/8 teaspoon freshly ground pepper

Combine the tomato, cucumbers, green onion tops, capers, vinegar, lemon juice, salt and pepper in a bowl and mix well. Let stand at room temperature for 1 hour. Strain to remove the excess liquid.

Makes 3/4 cup

Horseradish Cream Sauce

1/4 cup sour cream
1 teaspoon horseradish

Combine the sour cream and horseradish in a bowl and mix well.

Makes 1/4 cup

Cilantro Lime Vinaigrette

1/2 cup olive oil
1/2 cup vegetable oil
1/4 cup fresh lime juice
6 tablespoons chopped fresh cilantro
2 tablespoons ground cumin

1 teaspoon grated lime zest
1 teaspoon minced jalapeño chile
1 teaspoon salt
1/4 teaspoon freshly ground pepper

Combine the olive oil, vegetable oil, lime juice, cilantro, cumin, lime zest, jalapeño chile, salt and pepper in a bowl and blend well.

Makes 2 cups

Exotic Greens with Strawberry Vinaigrette

Strawberry Vinaigrette
8 ounces frozen strawberries
1/4 cup sugar
1 teaspoon balsamic vinegar
1 teaspoon rice wine vinegar
1/3 cup olive oil
1/3 cup soybean oil
1/2 teaspoon salt
1/4 teaspoon white pepper

Salad
8 cups baby salad greens
1 cup chopped tomato
1/4 cup pine nuts, toasted
6 whole strawberries, fanned
2 ounces goat cheese

For the vinaigrette, process the strawberries in a blender until puréed. Add the sugar, balsamic vinegar, rice wine vinegar, olive oil, soybean oil, salt and white pepper and process until blended.

For the salad, toss the salad greens and tomato with the vinaigrette in a salad bowl to coat. Place on six chilled salad plates. Top with the pine nuts, strawberries and goat cheese.

Serves 6

Rack of Lamb with Two Sauces

1 (2-pound) rack of lamb
Kosher salt to taste
Coarse pepper to taste
Port Wine and Balsamic Vinegar Sauce (page 23)
English Mint Sauce (below)
Herb-Roasted Vegetables (page 24)
Roasted Red Potatoes (page 24)

Preheat the oven to 400 degrees. Remove the excess fat from the rack of lamb and season with kosher salt and pepper. Place on a rack in a roasting pan. Bake until the fat begins to turn a golden brown. Reduce the oven temperature to 300 degrees. Continue to roast the lamb to the desired degree of doneness. Remove from the oven and let stand for 5 minutes before carving. The internal temperature may increase an additional 10 degrees.

To serve, place the rack of lamb with the fat side down on a cutting board. Cut between each bone to separate the chops. Stack the chops in the center of each serving plate. Spoon 1 tablespoon port wine and balsamic vinegar sauce at the top of each plate and spoon 1 tablespoon mint sauce at the bottom of each plate. Place the vegetables and potatoes on either side of the chops.

Serves 4

English Mint Sauce

1/4 cup sugar
2 tablespoons warm water
1/4 cup white wine vinegar
1/2 cup balsamic vinegar
3/4 cup fresh mint, chopped

Dissolve the sugar in the warm water in a bowl. Stir in the white wine vinegar, balsamic vinegar and mint. Cover and chill in the refrigerator.

Serves 8

Port Wine and Balsamic Vinegar Sauce

1/4 cup port
4 cups Quick Beef Stock (below) or
  canned beef stock
2 teaspoons balsamic vinegar
1 teaspoon salt

1/4 teaspoon white pepper
Pinch of cayenne pepper
1 teaspoon soy sauce
1/4 cup cornstarch
1/4 cup water

Heat the wine in a small saucepan until reduced by one-half. Add the stock, vinegar, salt, white pepper, cayenne pepper and soy sauce and bring to a boil. Dissolve the cornstarch in the water to make a slurry for thickening. Whisk the slurry vigorously into the boiling stock. Reduce the heat and simmer for 20 minutes to incorporate the starch.

Makes 4 cups

Quick Beef Stock

2 pounds beef scraps or beef neck
  bones
4 yellow onions, sliced
2 ribs celery, sliced
2 carrots, coarsely chopped
5 garlic cloves, crushed
1/4 cup canola oil
1/2 cup tomato paste
2 cups marsala
1 gallon water
2 cups sliced mushrooms

5 dried shiitake mushrooms
2 dried bay leaves
2 sprigs of fresh thyme
2 teaspoons dried rosemary
1 teaspoon dried marjoram
2 allspice berries, or 1/4 teaspoon dried
  allspice
1/2 teaspoon freshly ground pepper
2 tablespoons salt
2 tablespoons soy sauce

Preheat the oven to 400 degrees. Roast the beef scraps in a roasting pan until dark brown. Sauté the onions, celery, carrots and garlic in the canola oil in a large sauté pan until brown. Stir in the tomato paste and continue to sauté. Add 1 cup of the wine and simmer. Add the remaining 1 cup wine and stir to deglaze the pan. Simmer until the mixture is reduced by one-third. Add the water, roasted beef bones, sliced mushrooms, shiitake mushrooms, bay leaves, thyme, rosemary, marjoram, allspice berries, pepper, salt and soy sauce. Simmer for 1 1/2 hours. Strain the stock, discarding the solids. Store the stock in the refrigerator until ready to use.

Makes 1 gallon

Herb-Roasted Vegetables

1/4 cup sliced carrots
1/4 cup coarsely chopped zucchini
1/4 cup julienned red onion
1/2 teaspoon chopped fresh rosemary
Salt and pepper to taste
1 teaspoon olive oil

Preheat the oven to 300 degrees. Combine the carrots, zucchini, onion, rosemary, salt, pepper and olive oil in a large bowl and toss to mix. Place in a baking pan. Roast for 20 minutes, stirring every 5 minutes.

Note: You may roast the vegetables in the same oven with the Rack of Lamb on page 22.

Serves 4

Roasted Red Potatoes

2 pounds red potatoes, cut into wedges
1 teaspoon chopped fresh rosemary
1/4 cup olive oil
1 teaspoon salt
1/4 teaspoon freshly ground pepper

Preheat the oven to 300 degrees. Combine the red potatoes, rosemary, olive oil, salt and pepper in a bowl and toss to coat. Place in a baking pan. Roast for 25 minutes, stirring occasionally.

Note: You may roast the potatoes in the same oven with the Rack of Lamb on page 22.

Serves 4

Arizona Cream with Raspberry Purée

1¹/2 tablespoons unflavored gelatin
2 cups nonfat milk
1¹/4 cups sugar
1¹/2 tablespoons honey
2 teaspoons vanilla extract
4 cups nonfat plain yogurt
Juice and grated zest of 1 lemon
Nutmeg to taste
8 ounces frozen raspberries
Sugar to taste

Soften the gelatin in the milk in a double boiler. Add 1¹/4 cups sugar, the honey and vanilla and mix well. Heat to 180 degrees on a candy thermometer. Remove from the heat and cool to 100 degrees. Combine with the yogurt in a large bowl. Stir in the lemon juice, lemon zest and nutmeg. Pour into serving glasses and chill for several hours.

Process the raspberries in a food processor until puréed and add sugar to taste. Spoon over the top of the cream and serve.

Serves 8

Mojitos

2 cups light rum
1 cup Mint Syrup (below)
1 cup lime juice
2 cups (about) ice cubes

Combine the rum, mint syrup and lime juice in a 2-quart pitcher and stir to blend. Add about 2 cups ice cubes. Pour into ice-filled glasses and garnish with fresh mint leaves.

Serves 6 to 8

Mint Syrup

1¹/4 cups tightly packed rinsed fresh mint leaves
1 cup water
¹/2 cup sugar

Combine the mint leaves, water and sugar in a 1- or 2-quart saucepan. Cook over medium heat until the sugar is dissolved and the mixture simmers, stirring constantly. Remove the saucepan from the heat. Cover and let stand for 30 minutes. Pour the mixture through a fine strainer into a small pitcher or bowl, discarding the mint leaves. Use the syrup or cover and store in the refrigerator for up to 1 week.

Makes 1 cup

Stuffed Mushrooms

2 pounds large mushrooms
2 tablespoons butter, melted
2 teaspoons minced garlic
8 ounces cream cheese, softened
1 teaspoon granulated garlic
1/4 teaspoon dried dill weed
2 to 3 tablespoons grated Parmesan cheese
2 to 3 tablespoons dry bread crumbs
Salt and pepper to taste
2 tablespoons grated Parmesan cheese
2 tablespoons dry bread crumbs

Preheat the oven to 400 degrees. Rinse the mushrooms and pat dry. Remove the stems and reserve. Place the mushroom caps on a baking sheet and brush with 1 tablespoon of the melted butter. Bake for 8 to 10 minutes or until tender. Drain and cool. Maintain the oven temperature.

Chop the reserved mushroom stems. Sauté the chopped mushroom stems and minced garlic in the remaining 1 tablespoon butter in a skillet. Remove from the heat to cool. Add the cream cheese and mix thoroughly. Add the granulated garlic, dill weed, 2 to 3 tablespoons Parmesan cheese and 2 to 3 tablespoons bread crumbs and mix well. Season with salt and pepper. Spoon into a pastry bag fitted with a star tip and pipe into the mushroom caps. Sprinkle with 2 tablespoons Parmesan cheese and 2 tablespoons bread crumbs. Bake for 5 to 7 minutes or until brown.

Note: You may prepare the day before and store in the refrigerator until ready to bake.

Serves 8 to 10

Crab Cakes with Corn Sauce

Corn Sauce
- 1/2 cup marsala
- 2 tablespoons chopped shallots
- 2 teaspoons salt
- 1/4 teaspoon white pepper
- 3 cups whipping cream
- 1/2 cup water
- 1 cup roasted corn kernels or frozen roasted corn kernels, thawed
- 1/4 cup all-purpose flour
- 2 tablespoons butter, melted

Crab Cakes
- 1 pound crab meat, shells removed and crab meat flaked
- 1 rib celery, chopped (about 1/2 cup)
- 1/4 cup chopped red bell pepper
- 1 cup fresh corn kernels or frozen corn kernels, thawed
- 1 teaspoon horseradish
- 1 1/2 teaspoons Dijon mustard
- 1 tablespoon lemon juice
- 1 teaspoon grated lemon zest
- 2 tablespoons chopped fresh chives
- 1/2 teaspoon salt
- 1/4 teaspoon freshly ground black pepper
- Pinch of cayenne pepper
- 2 cups panko (Japanese bread crumbs)
- 2 eggs
- 1/2 cup Clarified Butter (page 29)

For the corn sauce, bring the wine, shallots, salt and white pepper to a boil in a large saucepan. Cook until the mixture is reduced by one-half. Add the cream and water and return to a boil. Stir in the corn. Mix the flour and butter together and whisk into the boiling sauce. Reduce the heat and simmer for 20 minutes. Pour into a blender and process until puréed. Adjust the seasonings to taste and strain into a bowl. Keep warm.

For the crab cakes, combine the crab meat, celery, bell pepper, corn, horseradish, Dijon mustard, lemon juice, lemon zest, chives, salt, black pepper, cayenne pepper, 1/2 cup of the panko, 1/2 cup of the corn sauce and the eggs in a large bowl and mix thoroughly. Adjust the seasonings to taste. Divide the crab meat mixture into sixteen 2-ounce balls. Gently shape each ball into a round cake about 1/2 inch thick. Dredge the crab cakes in the remaining 1 1/2 cups panko, gently pressing to adhere. Heat a large skillet over high heat. Cover the bottom of the skillet with the clarified butter. Add the crab cakes and fry for 2 to 3 minutes per side or until golden brown. Drain on paper towels.

To serve, ladle 1/4 cup of the remaining corn sauce on each serving plate and place the crab cakes in the pool of sauce.

Makes 16 appetizer-size crab cakes

Tiropitas

8 ounces cream cheese, softened
4 ounces goat cheese
1/4 cup finely chopped fresh chives
1 (16-ounce) package phyllo
Hot Clarified Butter (below)

Combine the cream cheese, goat cheese and chives in a mixing bowl and mix well. Unfold the phyllo onto a large cutting board and cut into 2-inch strips. Stack all of the strips in a pile beside the cutting board and keep covered with a damp towel to prevent drying out. Place three individual strips of phyllo side by side on the cutting board and brush with clarified butter. Cover these strips with another individual layer of phyllo and brush with clarified butter. Repeat until the three stacks have four layers each.

Place a teaspoon of the cream cheese filling near the end of each set of phyllo strips. Fold the left corner of the phyllo diagonally over the filling to form a triangle and seal the seam with clarified butter. Fold the right corner up and over the filling and brush the top of the triangle and edge with the clarified butter. Repeat this process until you reach the end of the strip, folding the last flap around the tiropita and brushing the entire outside surface with the clarified butter. Repeat with the remaining phyllo strips, filling and clarified butter. Store the tiropitas in a freezer container with waxed paper between each layer.

To serve, preheat the oven to 400 degrees. Place the frozen tiropitas on a baking sheet. Bake for 3 minutes per side or until golden brown.

Makes about 35

Clarified Butter

1 pound butter

Melt the butter in a small saucepan and bring to a boil. Reduce the heat and simmer for 5 minutes. Some of the milk solids will rise to the top and some will collect on the bottom of the pan. Skim the solids from the surface. Pour the clarified butter slowly off the top, leaving the white milk solids in the bottom of the pan. Chill the clarified butter until solidified. Cut into cubes and store in the refrigerator or freezer.

Makes 1 1/3 cups

EL TOVAR
"We're Not Just Close, We're There"

Built by the Santa Fe Railroad in 1905, El Tovar provided premiere accommodations on the south rim of Grand Canyon at the end of an 80-mile railroad spur from Williams, Arizona. Construction costs were $250,000 when it opened with 95 rooms and seven bathrooms—one per wing. Electricity and telephones were installed in every room. Eventually reducing total guest rooms to 78, along with another 12 suites, a bathroom was added to each accommodation.

El Tovar was designed by Illinois architect Charles Whittlesey, who combined the elegance of a European villa with the look of an American hunting lodge. Its name was derived from Spanish explorer Don Pedro de Tovar of Coronado's expedition, who first reported the existence of Grand Canyon.

Architect Mary Elizabeth Jane Colter chose the site just opposite El Tovar to build the stunning Hopi House that also opened in 1905. Constructed as a trading post in the style of a Hopi pueblo and using Hopi craftsmen, it was patterned after Oraibi Village on Third Mesa. Today, it showcases and offers for sale genuine handcrafted Indian goods.

Each structure complements the other. These two architectural jewels combined with the entrepreneurial genius of Fred Harvey and his hospitable food service; it's no wonder early guests often stayed for weeks at a time.

El Tovar celebrated its centennial in 2005, reopening after a $4.8 million renovation in those sections of the building not considered historic. The lobby, today, looks exactly as it did in 1905 when El Tovar welcomed its first guests. Its ceiling towers high above with exposed Oregon pine logs and copper chandeliers. Old buffalo heads, rumored to have been shot by President Teddy Roosevelt, stare down upon hotel visitors. Comfortable leather furniture, Indian artifacts and Thomas Moran paintings encourage guests' closer inspections. A massive stone fireplace still dominates El Tovar's wonderfully rustic yet formal dining room.

El Tovar and Hopi House are Registered National Historic Landmarks. Owner Xanterra, L.L.C., has retained El Tovar's historic elegance and charm for today's visitors to enjoy.

Luncheon Menu

Tortilla Soup
◆ Salmon Tostada
Apple Pie

Dinner Menu

Salad of Field Greens
◆ Pork Chop with Chorizo Black Bean Stuffing
◆ Green Chile Grits
◆ Mélange of Sautéed Vegetables
◆ Blackberry Linzer Tart

◆ *Recipes Included*

El Tovar

Salmon Tostada

4 (6-inch) blue corn tortillas
4 (6-inch) corn tortillas
Vegetable oil for frying
2 cups Roasted Pistachio Rice (below)
2 to 3 cups spring salad mix
1/2 cup Tequila Vinaigrette (page 33)

4 (4-ounce) wild salmon
  fillets, skinned
Salt and pepper to taste
1 cup Corn Salsa (page 33)
1/2 cup sour cream
3 tablespoons fresh lime juice

Fry the tortillas in oil in a skillet and place one of each kind in the center of each of four bowls. Spoon 1/2 cup of the rice in the center of each bowl. Toss the salad mix with the vinaigrette in a salad bowl to coat and place over the rice. Season the fish with salt and pepper and sear in a skillet. Place over the salad mix. Spoon the salsa over the fish. Whisk the sour cream and lime juice in a bowl until blended and drizzle over the top. Garnish each serving with a sprig of fresh cilantro.

Serves 4

Roasted Pistachio Rice

1/2 cup finely chopped yellow onion
1/4 cup finely chopped red bell pepper
1/4 cup finely chopped green bell
  pepper
1/2 carrot, finely chopped
2 tablespoons canola oil
1 garlic clove, chopped

2 tablespoons chopped cilantro
2 cups cooked rice
2 tablespoons butter, cut into cubes
Salt and pepper to taste
3/4 cup pistachio nuts, toasted
  and chopped

Sauté the onion, bell peppers and carrot in the canola oil in a sauté pan until the onion is translucent. Add the garlic and cilantro and sauté for 3 minutes. Stir in the cooked rice. Add the butter and heat until melted, stirring constantly. Season with salt and pepper. Fold in the pistachio nuts.

Makes 2 cups

Tequila Vinaigrette

3/4 cup tequila
3/4 cup vegetable oil
2 teaspoons chopped garlic
1/4 cup cilantro, chopped
3 tablespoons honey

2 tablespoons prickly pear syrup
1/4 cup apple cider vinegar
1 teaspoon freshly ground pepper
1/2 teaspoon salt

Cook the tequila in a saucepan until reduced to 1/4 cup. Process the reduced tequila, oil, garlic, cilantro, honey, prickly pear syrup, vinegar, pepper and salt in a blender until emulsified.

Makes 1 1/2 cups

Corn Salsa

1 or 2 jalapeño chiles, seeded
    and minced
1 1/2 cups roasted corn
    (about 2 large ears)
1/4 cup finely chopped green
    bell pepper
1/4 cup finely chopped red bell pepper

1 tablespoon chopped fresh cilantro
1/2 red onion, finely chopped
1 tomato, chopped
1 tablespoon sugar
1/2 cup vegetable juice cocktail
1 tablespoon lime juice
Salt to taste

Combine the jalapeño chiles, corn, bell peppers, cilantro, onion, tomato, sugar, vegetable juice cocktail, lime juice and salt in a large bowl and toss to mix.

Makes 3 1/2 cups

Pork Chop with Chorizo Black Bean Stuffing

1/4 cup finely chopped yellow onion
1/2 carrot, finely chopped
1/2 rib celery, finely chopped
1 tablespoon olive oil
1 garlic clove, minced
1/2 cup chorizo
1/2 cup (2 ounces) shredded Monterey
  Jack cheese
1/4 cup heavy cream
1/2 cup bread crumbs
1/2 cup drained, rinsed canned
  black beans

1/2 teaspoon hand-ground whole leaf
  oregano
Salt and pepper to taste
6 (1 1/2-inch-thick) rib pork chops
  with pockets
3/4 cup Prickly Pear Barbecue Sauce
  (page 36)
Green Chile Grits (page 36)
Mélange of Sautéed Vegetables
  (page 36)

Sauté the onion, carrot and celery in the olive oil in a skillet over medium heat until the onion is translucent. Add the garlic and sauté for 2 minutes. Add the chorizo and sauté for 3 minutes. Remove from the heat and stir in the cheese and cream. Add the bread crumbs, black beans, oregano, salt and pepper and stir to mix well. Cool to room temperature.

Preheat the oven to 350 degrees. Stuff the pork chops with the black bean mixture. Sauté in a skillet until brown and place in a baking pan. Bake until the internal temperature of the pork chops registers 155 degrees on a meat thermometer. Spoon 2 tablespoons of the barbecue sauce into the center of each serving plate and place a stuffed pork chop in the center of the barbecue sauce. Spoon the grits in the position of twelve o'clock and six o'clock on each plate. Spoon the vegetables in the position of nine o'clock and three o'clock on each plate.

Serves 6

Prickly Pear Barbecue Sauce

1/2 cup prickly pear syrup
1/4 cup tomato paste
1/2 teaspoon fresh lemon juice

1 1/2 teaspoons ancho chile powder
1 teaspoon onion powder
Salt to taste

Combine the prickly pear syrup, tomato paste, lemon juice, ancho chile powder, onion powder and salt in a bowl and mix well.

Makes 3/4 cup

Green Chile Grits

1 cup quick-cooking grits
Salt and pepper to taste
1/4 cup chopped mild green chiles

1/2 cup (2 ounces) shredded sharp
    Cheddar cheese

Prepare the grits using the package directions, seasoning with salt and pepper. Remove from the heat and stir in the green chiles and cheese.

Serves 6

Mélange of Sautéed Vegetables

4 yellow squash, chopped
4 zucchini, chopped
12 baby carrots, or 1/2 cup
    sliced carrots

1 red bell pepper, julienned
1/4 cup (1/2 stick) butter
Salt and freshly ground pepper to taste

Sauté the squash, zucchini, carrots and bell pepper in 2 tablespoons of the butter in a sauté pan over medium heat until tender-crisp. Top with the remaining 2 tablespoons butter and season with salt and pepper.

Serves 6

Blackberry Linzer Tart

1¹/4 cups all-purpose flour
¹/2 teaspoon ground cinnamon
¹/4 teaspoon salt
1¹/4 cups (2¹/2 sticks) butter, softened
1 cup granulated sugar
2 eggs
1¹/4 cups hazelnuts, ground
²/3 cup blackberry preserves
1 egg
2 tablespoons water
¹/4 cup heavy whipping cream
2 tablespoons confectioners' sugar
¹/4 teaspoon vanilla extract

Sift the flour, cinnamon and salt together. Cream the butter and granulated sugar in a bowl of a stand mixer until light and fluffy. Add two eggs and beat well. Add the hazelnuts and flour mixture and mix well. Divide the pastry into two equal portions. Pat one portion of the pastry into the bottom of a 9-inch tart pan with a removable bottom. Spread the preserves to within ¹/2 inch of the side. Chill the remaining pastry for 30 minutes before using.

Preheat the oven to 325 degrees. Roll the chilled pastry into a circle on a lightly floured surface. Cut into strips and arrange in a lattice pattern on top of the preserves. Brush with a mixture of one egg and the water. Bake on the middle oven rack for 30 to 40 minutes or until the lattice is evenly brown. Remove from the oven to cool.

Whip the cream with 1 tablespoon of the confectioners' sugar and the vanilla in the mixing bowl of a stand mixer until soft peaks form. Place in a pastry bag fitted with a star tip and pipe rosettes around the tart. Sprinkle with the remaining 1 tablespoon confectioners' sugar.

Serves 8

GARLAND'S OAK CREEK LODGE
"It's the Prettiest Spot in Arizona"

The Lodge started with a pine log structure in 1908, using trees felled from the hills above the property. It wasn't easy. Oak Creek was homesteaded the hard way, packing in all supplies by horseback because there was no road. After changing hands several times, the property was purchased in the late 1920s by Frank and Catherine Todd and their son Bill.

Cabins were built, two by two, and Todd's Lodge became a treasured getaway for miners from Jerome and locals from Flagstaff. Simple and appetizing meals were served family style.

The Bill and Georgiana Garland family were regular Oak Creek visitors during the hot Phoenix summers, and longtime friends of the Todds when they bought the property from them in 1972. They were committed to keeping the spirit of the Lodge unchanged. With children Gary, Susan and Dan, the Garlands built more cabins and remodeled older structures. Bill expanded the business, opening Garland's Navajo Rugs and Jewelry and the Indian Gardens Trading Post, while son Gary with his wife, Mary, operate the Lodge.

The original pine building is now the kitchen where their chef of 25 years, Amanda Stine, creates superb gourmet meals for today's fashionable clientele. Meals included are breakfast, afternoon tea and dinner. Count on enjoying vegetables from Garland's garden, fruit from the orchard, eggs from their chickens and honey from their hives.

National travel and entertaining authorities recognize Garland's for its scenic location and "glorious food." These include *Travel and Leisure*, *National Geographic Traveler*, *Food and Wine*, and Martha Stewart's *Entertaining*.

BREAKFAST MENU

Fresh Apple Cider

Granola

◆ Swiss Baked Eggs

◆ Stewed Dried Plums

Crisp Bacon or Sausages

◆ Sour Cream Muffins

DINNER MENU

◆ Red Lentil Chowder

◆ Mixed Greens with Pears, Roquefort and Pecans
with Celery Seed Vinaigrette

◆ Roast Pork Tenderloin with Rhubarb Pear Chutney
and Pinot Demi-Glace

Mushroom Wild Rice Pilaf

◆ Rosemary Raisin Bread

◆ Garland's Apple Tart

◆ *Recipes Included*

Garland's Oak Creek Lodge

Swiss Baked Eggs

3 cups (12 ounces) shredded Swiss cheese
6 eggs
6 tablespoons heavy cream
2 tablespoons chopped chives
3/8 teaspoon salt
3/8 teaspoon white pepper
3/8 teaspoon ground nutmeg (optional)
Butter
6 English muffin halves, toasted
6 slices ham or Canadian bacon, lightly fried

Preheat the oven to 350 degrees. Spray six individual baking dishes or 1/2-cup ramekins with nonstick cooking spray. Line each dish with 1/4 cup of the shredded cheese and make wells in the cheese. Carefully crack and place one egg in each well. Spoon 1 tablespoon of the cream over each yolk. Sprinkle 1 teaspoon chives, a pinch of salt, a pinch of white pepper and a pinch of nutmeg over each dish. Sprinkle each with the remaining cheese. Place a small dab of butter on top of the cheese. Bake for 15 minutes or until set. Remove from the oven and loosen from the side of each dish. Place the English muffin halves on individual serving plates and top with a slice of ham. Invert the egg mixture on top of the ham and serve immediately.

Serves 6

Stewed Dried Plums

2 oranges
2 pounds pitted dried plums (prunes)
2 cups orange juice

1 cup tawny port
10 to 12 cinnamon sticks

Cut the unpeeled oranges into 1/2-inch slices. Cut each slice into halves and remove the seeds. Combine the oranges, plums, orange juice, wine and cinnamon sticks in a heavy nonreactive saucepan. Cover and bring to a boil. Reduce the heat and uncover. Simmer over low heat for 1 to 2 minutes, stirring gently. Remove from the heat and let stand to plump the plums, stirring gently every 10 minutes or until cool. The juices will thicken as the plums cool and will form a nice glaze. Serve warm, making sure each serving has two half slices of orange and a cinnamon stick. Garnish with fresh mint.

Note: Any remaining stewed plums will keep for weeks in the refrigerator. Cool before refrigerating and reheat before serving as they are most flavorful when warm.

Serves 12

Sour Cream Muffins

2 cups all-purpose flour
1 tablespoon baking powder
1/4 teaspoon salt
1/2 cup sugar

1 egg
1/4 cup canola oil
1 1/2 cups sour cream

Preheat the oven to 400 degrees. Sift the flour, baking powder, salt and sugar together into a medium bowl and make a well in the center. Beat the egg and canola oil in a mixing bowl. Stir in the sour cream. Spoon into the well in the flour mixture and mix until the batter sticks together and resembles biscuit dough. Do not overmix. Spoon into muffin cups sprayed with nonstick cooking spray. Bake for 20 to 25 minutes or until golden brown.

Variations:

For Lemon Blueberry Sour Cream Muffins, fold in 1 cup blueberries and 1 to 2 teaspoons grated lemon zest.

For Cranberry Sour Cream Muffins, plump 1 cup dried cranberries in orange juice and drain well. Fold in the cranberries, 1 teaspoon grated orange zest and 1 cup chopped walnuts.

Serves 12

Red Lentil Chowder

2 to 3 ribs celery, sliced
  (about 1¹/₂ cups)
2 carrots, sliced (about 1¹/₂ cups)
1 yellow onion, chopped
  (about 1¹/₂ cups)
1 tablespoon minced garlic
1 teaspoon minced fresh ginger
1 teaspoon kosher salt
2 tablespoons olive oil
1 teaspoon dried leaf thyme
1 teaspoon dried marjoram
1 teaspoon ground cinnamon
2 teaspoons coriander

1¹/₂ teaspoons cumin
¹/₄ teaspoon cayenne pepper
1 cup chopped canned pear tomatoes
1¹/₂ cups dried red lentils, rinsed
8 cups water, or 4 cups chicken broth
  and 4 cups water
1¹/₂ cups ¹/₂-inch pieces butternut
  squash or other winter squash
2 to 3 tablespoons chopped
  fresh cilantro
Salt and pepper to taste
2 tablespoons fresh lemon juice,
  or to taste

Sauté the celery, carrots, onion, garlic, ginger and kosher salt in the olive oil in a
4- to 6-quart stockpot over medium heat. Cover and sweat for 5 minutes. Add the thyme,
marjoram, cinnamon, coriander, cumin, cayenne pepper and tomatoes. Cover and sweat
for 1 to 2 minutes. Add the lentils and water and stir to mix well. Cover and bring to a
gentle boil. Reduce the heat and simmer for 15 minutes. Add the squash. Cook for 15 to
20 minutes or until the lentils and the vegetables are tender. Stir in the cilantro, salt, pepper
and lemon juice. You may add an additional 1 cup water if the chowder is too thick.

Note: Sweating is cooking a food (typically vegetables) in a small amount of fat, usually
covered, over low heat without browning until the food softens and releases moisture.
Sweating allows the food to release its flavor more quickly when it is later cooked with
other foods.

Serves 8 to 10

Mixed Greens with Pears, Roquefort and Pecans with Celery Seed Vinaigrette

Celery Seed Vinaigrette

1/3 cup raspberry white wine vinegar
2 tablespoons sugar
1/2 teaspoon dry mustard
1 tablespoon chopped yellow onion
1/2 teaspoon salt
1/3 cup walnut oil
1/3 cup canola oil
1/2 teaspoon celery seeds

Salad

1 cup pecans, chopped
1 teaspoon extra-virgin olive oil
1/2 teaspoon salt
4 large red Bartlett pears or Anjou pears
4 quarts mixed salad greens, rinsed and spun dry
1 cup crumbled Roquefort cheese

For the vinaigrette, combine the vinegar, sugar, dry mustard, onion, salt, walnut oil, canola oil and celery seeds in a 2-cup glass measure and blend until smooth. Use a hand-held blender, if desired.

For the salad, preheat the oven to 325 degrees. Toss the pecans with the olive oil and salt in a bowl and spread on a baking sheet. Bake for 8 to 10 minutes or until toasted. Pour 1/3 cup of the vinaigrette into a 1-quart bowl. Quarter and core one pear at a time and slice each quarter lengthwise into 1/4-inch wedges into the vinaigrette. Cover and chill until ready to serve. Place the mixed salad greens in a large bowl and toss with the remaining vinaigrette. Divide among eight salad plates. Sprinkle the cheese around the salad greens. Arrange five pear wedges on each salad and sprinkle with the toasted pecans.

Serves 8

Roast Pork Tenderloin with Rhubarb Pear Chutney and Pinot Demi-Glace

Herb Spice Rub
2 tablespoons fennel seeds
2 tablespoons mustard seeds
2 tablespoons dried oregano
2 tablespoons dried thyme
2 tablespoons dried sage
2 tablespoons chopped fresh rosemary
Zest of 1 orange
1/2 cup salt
1/4 cup freshly ground coarse pepper

Pork
4 (1- to 1 1/2-pound) pork tenderloins
Olive oil
Pinot Demi-Glace (page 46)
Rhubarb Pear Chutney (page 46)

For the rub, toast the fennel seeds, mustard seeds, oregano, thyme, sage, rosemary and orange zest in a small skillet until fragrant. Grind in a spice mill or coffee grinder. Mix with the salt and pepper in a bowl.

For the pork, brush the pork with a small amount of olive oil and sprinkle the rub over the surface. Place on a rack in a roasting pan. Let stand for 30 minutes. Preheat the oven to 350 degrees. Roast the pork on the upper oven rack for 8 minutes. Reduce the oven temperature to 300 degrees. Roast for 8 to 10 minutes longer or until an instant-read meat thermometer registers 140 degrees. Do not overcook. The pork should be firm but yield to a gentle squeeze. Remove from the oven and cover with a clean towel. Let stand for 10 minutes. To serve, cut the pork into slices 1/3 inch thick and place on warm individual serving plates. Spoon about 1/4 cup of the demi-glace over each serving and top with 2 tablespoons of the chutney. Garnish with sprigs of fresh rosemary.

Note: Any remaining pinot demi-glace may be frozen, and the chutney can be stored in the refrigerator for up to 2 weeks.

Serves 8

Pinot Demi-Glace

1 cup chopped yellow onion
3 garlic cloves, chopped
2 tablespoons fresh thyme leaves,
    or 1 teaspoon dried thyme
2 tablespoons fresh sage leaves,
    or 1 teaspoon dried sage
1 teaspoon fresh coarsely
    ground pepper

1/2 teaspoon salt
1 tablespoon olive oil
3 cups pinot noir
3 cups rich beef stock or chicken stock
1 cup demi-glace base
1 to 2 teaspoons sugar, or to taste
Salt to taste

Sauté the onion, garlic, thyme, sage, pepper and 1/2 teaspoon salt in the olive oil in a heavy 3-quart saucepan over medium heat until golden brown. Add the wine and cook until the mixture is reduced by one-half. Add the stock and cook until reduced by one-third. Add the demi-glace base and cook until thickened and shiny. Strain the sauce into a clean small saucepan. Add the sugar to smooth it out. Adjust the salt to taste. Keep warm until ready to serve.

Makes 3 cups

Rhubarb Pear Chutney

1 cup minced red onion
4 garlic cloves, pressed
1 tablespoon minced ginger
1/4 cup orange juice
1/4 cup apple cider vinegar
1/3 cup sugar, or to taste
2 1/2 cups chopped rhubarb

2 1/2 cups chopped peeled pears
    or apples
1 cinnamon stick
1/4 teaspoon red pepper flakes,
    or to taste
1 teaspoon salt, or to taste

Combine the onion, garlic, ginger, orange juice, vinegar and 1/3 cup sugar in a heavy 3-quart saucepan. Cook over medium heat until the sugar dissolves and the onion softens. Stir in the rhubarb, pears, cinnamon stick, red pepper flakes and 1 teaspoon salt. Cook for 1 minute. Remove from the heat and keep in a warm place to let the flavors develop and soften. Adjust the salt and sugar to taste.

Makes 4 cups

Rosemary Raisin Bread

1 cup raisins
2 cups warm water
1 tablespoon dry yeast
1 cup warm water
1 cup warm milk
1/4 cup sugar
1 tablespoon salt

1 tablespoon chopped fresh
   rosemary leaves
3 eggs, beaten
1/4 cup olive oil
2 cups whole wheat flour
4 cups bread flour

Soak the raisins in 2 cups warm water in a bowl for 5 minutes to plump; drain well. Dissolve the yeast in 1 cup warm water. Combine the warm milk, sugar, salt and rosemary in a bowl of a stand mixer fitted with a dough hook. Add the beaten eggs and mix at low speed for 1 minute. Mix in the olive oil and then the yeast mixture. Add the whole wheat flour and 3 cups of the bread flour. Mix at low speed until the dough begins to come together. Add the remaining bread flour a small amount at a time, mixing at low speed until the dough forms a ball and leaves the side of the bowl. Add the well-drained raisins gradually, mixing constantly at low speed.

Place the dough in a lightly oiled large bowl. Cover with plastic wrap and let rise in a warm place for 2 hours or until doubled in bulk. Remove the plastic wrap and turn the dough onto a clean work surface. Lightly sprinkle flour over and around the dough and knead until smooth and elastic. Divide the dough into two equal portions and shape into a ball. Cover with plastic wrap and let rest for 10 minutes.

Press each portion into an 8×10-inch rectangle. Shape into loaves by rolling up the dough from the top of the rectangle towards you, pressing at the edge with your thumbs to seal. Place seam side down in two lightly oiled 5×9 inch loaf pans. Cover with plastic wrap and let rise in a warm place for 40 to 60 minutes or until doubled in bulk.

Preheat the oven to 350 degrees. Make three diagonal cuts in the top of each loaf and place on the middle oven rack. Bake for 40 to 50 minutes or until the tops are brown and the loaves sound hollow when tapped on the bottom. Cool completely on a wire rack.

Makes 2 loaves

Garland's Apple Tart

1 Tart Pastry (page 49)
3/4 cup all-purpose flour
1 cup packed brown sugar
1/2 cup (1 stick) cold butter,
    cut into cubes
1 cup sour cream
3/4 cup granulated sugar
2 tablespoons unbleached
    all-purpose flour

1/2 teaspoon salt
2 teaspoons vanilla extract
1 teaspoon ground cinnamon
1 egg
4 large or 5 medium Rome,
    MacIntosh, Jonathan or
    Granny Smith apples, peeled
    and sliced 1/4 inch thick

Preheat the oven to 450 degrees. Roll the pastry 1/8 to 1/4 inch thick on a lightly floured surface. Trim the edge into a large circle. Fold the circle in half gently and place over half of a 10-inch shallow fluted tart pan with a removable bottom. Unfold the dough and press over the bottom and up the side of the pan. Trim the excess dough around the edge, leaving 1/3 inch of the dough above the rim of the pan. Fold the edge down slightly so that it sits on the edge of the pan. Place the pan in the freezer for 5 minutes. Remove the tart shell from the freezer. Line with baking parchment paper or foil and fill with pie weights or dried beans. Bake for 12 to 15 minutes or until golden brown, removing the baking parchment paper and pie weights or dried beans a few minutes before the baking time is over.

Reduce the oven temperature to 375 degrees. Pulse 3/4 cup flour and the brown sugar in a food processor to blend. Add the butter cubes and pulse until the mixture resembles coarse cornmeal. Whisk the sour cream, granulated sugar, 2 tablespoons flour, the salt, vanilla, cinnamon and egg in a bowl until very smooth. Add the apple slices and mix gently to coat. Fill the cooled tart crust with the apple mixture just to the rim, spreading the apples evenly. Bake in the lower third of the oven for 20 to 25 minutes or just until the filling begins to set. Remove from the oven and spread the flour mixture evenly and completely over the top. Reduce the oven temperature to 350 degrees. Bake for 20 to 30 minutes or until the tart is a deep golden brown. Cool on a wire rack for 30 to 60 minutes before serving. Serve with vanilla ice cream.

Note: This tart is also good using pears or peaches.

Serves 12

Tart Pastry

3 cups unbleached all-purpose flour
1 teaspoon salt
2 tablespoons sugar
3/4 cup (1 1/2 sticks) unsalted butter, cut into pieces
1/2 cup plus 2 tablespoons shortening
1/4 cup cold water
1 tablespoon apple cider vinegar

Whisk the flour, salt and sugar lightly in a medium bowl to blend. Add the butter and shortening and toss lightly to coat. Cut with a pastry blender until the mixture resembles a very coarse cornmeal. Mix the water and vinegar together. Sprinkle about 3 tablespoons of the vinegar mixture over the flour mixture and toss to blend. Continue adding the vinegar mixture 1 tablespoon at a time, tossing to form a cohesive ball that will hold together when pressed. Divide the dough into two equal portions and shape each portion into a disk. Wrap and chill for at least 2 hours before using or store in the freezer.

Makes 2 pastry disks

HASSAYAMPA INN
"The Grand Dame of Prescott"

As early as 1920, Prescott's community leaders determined the need for a
first-class hotel in downtown Prescott. By 1925, Mayor Morris Goldwater urged local
citizens to invest in hotel stock through a public subscription of shares offered from one
dollar to $20 to raise money to build the grand dame of Prescott's historic district.

Henry C. Trost, an established and well-known El Paso architect, was selected
based on his previous work, the Carnegie Library in Tucson and the Gadsden Hotel in
Douglas. After the foundation was laid, Prescott locals challenged his previously
approved Pueblo Art Deco façade and he changed this to a simple brick design
reflecting the eastern and midwestern tastes of local residents.

Since the day in 1927 when the Hassayampa Inn opened its doors to those
seeking respite in the mile-high mountain oasis, the inn has been a retreat for travelers
desiring attentive service in a charming and laid-back environment. While the exterior was
changed to sensible brick, the interior exudes warmth and cheer of the romantic southwest.
Hand-painted ceiling beams, wall murals, rich, glazed tiles, etched and stained glass
windows and doors decry the compromise from a midwestern exterior to a
southwestern territorial interior. The old-fashioned gated elevator is still operated
by a specially licensed hotel employee.

The Hassayampa Inn is listed on the National Register of Historic Places and
is a member of the National Trust Historic Hotels of America.

BREAKFAST MENU

◆ Yogurt Parfaits

◆ Lemon Soufflé Pancakes

Crispy Bacon

◆ Sour Cream Pecan Coffee Cake

DINNER MENU

◆ Bruschetta

◆ Chicken Dijon

◆ Wild Rice Pilaf

◆ Summer Squash Sauté

Butter Pecan Ice Cream

Butter Cookies

◆ *Recipes Included*

Hassayampa Inn

Yogurt Parfaits

2 cups fresh blueberries
2 cups fresh raspberries
2 cups granola
Strawberry yogurt

Mix the blueberries and raspberries in a bowl. Alternate layers of the berries and granola in parfait glasses or wine glasses and top with the yogurt.

Note: You can use homemade or commercial granola and low-fat yogurt in this recipe if you prefer.

Serves 6

Lemon Soufflé Pancakes

10 egg whites
10 egg yolks
3/4 cup all-purpose flour
3 cups ricotta cheese
2 tablespoons butter, melted

1/3 cup sugar
Grated zest of 1 1/2 lemons
1 teaspoon salt
Vegetable oil

Beat the egg whites in a mixing bowl until stiff peaks form. Combine the egg yolks with the flour, ricotta cheese, butter, sugar, lemon zest and salt in a bowl and mix well. Fold in the egg whites gently, leaving small portions of egg white intact.

Preheat a griddle or skillet to medium-hot and brush with a small amount of vegetable oil. Spoon 3 tablespoons of the batter at a time onto the heated griddle and cook until bubbles appear. Turn the pancakes and cook until brown. Remove the pancakes to serving plates as they brown, allowing three pancakes for each serving. Serve with fresh raspberries and raspberry syrup.

Serves 6 (makes 18 pancakes)

Sour Cream Pecan Coffee Cake

Coffee Cake
  2 tablespoons butter, melted
  1/3 cup packed brown sugar
  1 tablespoon all-purpose flour
  1/4 teaspoon ground cinnamon
  1/4 cup pecans, chopped
  1 cup all-purpose flour
  1/4 teaspoon baking powder
  1/4 teaspoon baking soda
  1/4 teaspoon salt

  3 tablespoons butter, softened
  1/3 cup granulated sugar
  1 egg
  1 teaspoon vanilla extract
  1/2 cup sour cream

Confectioners' Sugar Icing
  1/4 cup confectioners' sugar
  2 teaspoons half-and-half

For the coffee cake, preheat the oven to 325 degrees. Mix 2 tablespoons butter, the brown sugar, 1 tablespoon flour, the cinnamon and pecans in a bowl. Sift 1 cup flour, the baking powder, baking soda and salt together. Cream 3 tablespoons butter and the granulated sugar in a mixing bowl until light and fluffy. Beat in the egg and vanilla. Add the sifted flour mixture alternately with the sour cream, mixing well after each addition.

Spoon into a buttered 8×8-inch baking pan and bake for 20 minutes. Sprinkle with the pecan mixture and bake for 15 minutes longer. Cool on a wire rack for 10 minutes.

For the icing, blend the confectioners' sugar and half-and-half in a bowl. Drizzle over the warm coffee cake.

Serves 8

Bruschetta

1 baguette
Olive oil for brushing
5 tomatoes, seeded and chopped
1 small red onion, finely chopped
1/4 cup fresh basil, finely chopped
1/2 cup (2 ounces) grated asiago cheese or
   Parmesan cheese
2 tablespoons olive oil
2 tablespoons white balsamic vinegar

Preheat the oven to 300 degrees. Cut the baguette into 1/2-inch slices. Brush the slices with olive oil and arrange on a baking sheet. Bake for 8 to 10 minutes or until golden brown.
Mix the tomatoes, onion, basil and cheese in a bowl. Add 2 tablespoons olive oil and the vinegar and mix well. Spoon onto the baguette slices and serve immediately.

Serves 8

Chicken Dijon

8 (8-ounce) boneless skinless
chicken breasts
2 cups heavy cream
1/4 cup Dijon mustard
1/4 cup Old-Style Dijon mustard
1 cup sliced mushrooms
Wild Rice Pilaf (page 57)
Summer Squash Sauté (page 57)

Pound the chicken breasts lightly. Grill or broil in the oven until cooked through. Keep warm.

Combine the cream, Dijon mustards and mushrooms in a saucepan and mix well. Cook over medium heat until reduced by one-half.

Spoon the pilaf onto the centers of eight serving plates and top with the chicken. Spoon the mushroom mixture over the chicken. Spoon the squash in the position of twelve o'clock, three o'clock, six o'clock and nine o'clock around the pilaf and chicken on the plates.

Serves 8

Wild Rice Pilaf

1 rib celery, finely chopped
1 large carrot, finely chopped
1 small onion, finely chopped
1 tablespoon minced garlic
3/4 cup chicken broth

2 cups cooked white rice
Salt to taste
3 cups water
1 cup uncooked wild rice
Pepper to taste

Combine the celery, carrot, onion and garlic with the broth in a saucepan. Cook over medium heat until the liquid has evaporated and the vegetables are tender. Stir in the white rice.

Bring the salted water to a boil in a saucepan. Add the wild rice and cover. Bring to a boil and reduce the heat to low. Simmer for 55 minutes or until tender; drain. Add the white rice mixture and mix gently. Season with salt and pepper.

Serves 8

Summer Squash Sauté

1 1/2 tablespoons unsalted butter
2 large summer squash, chopped
2 large red bell peppers, chopped

1 red onion, chopped
Salt and freshly ground pepper to taste

Melt the butter in a skillet and add the squash, bell peppers, and onion. Sauté until tender-crisp. Season with salt and pepper.

Serves 8

La Posada
"The Last Great Railroad Hotel"

Architect Mary Elizabeth Jane Colter was hired by Fred Harvey and the
Santa Fe Railroad to design La Posada in Winslow. In addition to overseeing construction
to create a fabulous Spanish Hacienda, Miss Colter also decorated the interiors and planned
the gardens. Construction costs in 1929 exceeded $1 million; museum quality furnishings,
gardens and landscaping added an additional million. La Posada opened
in 1930, seven months after the 1929 stock market crash, with 70 guest rooms,
three dining rooms and grand public space.

America's love of the automobile and the decline of railroad travel closed La Posada
in 1957, when it was converted to offices, destroying the original layout and
the hotel's historic charm.

Today's owner, Allan Affeldt, read that La Posada was designated an endangered piece
of historical architecture. Former member of a California think tank, Affeldt called the
Winslow Chamber of Commerce, made the deal, and began to renovate and restore the
last and most elegant of the Fred Harvey hotels. La Posada now has 38 restored
guest rooms, grand public space, a restaurant, the Turquoise Room
(named after the famous Santa Fe dining car) and Martini Bar.

Before Fred Harvey, "the Civilizer of the West," railroad travel was grim and
food stops offered inedible dry biscuits, greasy ham leather and weak coffee at fleecing
prices. Harvey changed that by building spotless dining rooms with good cooking
served by his "Harvey Girls." Aboard the train, the conductor collected food orders for
the counter or dining room and wired them ahead to ensure prompt service at the next
Harvey House stop. Early meals included a selection of seven entrées, with seconds, for
75 cents, increasing to one dollar in 1927, with a guaranteed 30-minute service time.

Original Fred Harvey recipes will give the reader a taste of the appetizing food
train travelers enjoyed during La Posada's heyday.

FRED HARVEY DINNER MENU

- ◆ Sherried Shrimp with Capers
- ◆ Scallopini of Veal Marsala
- ◆ Risotto Piedmontaise
- Baked Tomatoes
- ◆ Blueberry Muffins La Posada
- Corn Bread
- ◆ Brandy Flip Pie

◆ *Recipes Included*

La Posada Hotel

Sherried Shrimp with Capers

12 (1¹/2-ounce) shrimp, peeled
   and deveined
All-purpose flour for coating
1 garlic clove, minced
¹/2 cup (1 stick) butter

2 teaspoons fresh lemon juice
2 teaspoons capers
¹/4 cup dry sherry
Salt and pepper to taste

Coat the shrimp lightly with flour, shaking off the excess. Sauté the shrimp and garlic in the butter in a skillet for 2 minutes. Stir in the lemon juice and capers. Remove from the heat and add the sherry. Ignite the sherry; allow the flames to subside. Sauté for 30 seconds longer. Season with salt and pepper.

Serves 4

Scallopini of Veal Marsala

2 pounds veal steak
1 small onion, finely chopped
1 garlic clove, minced
2 tablespoons butter
2 tablespoons all-purpose flour

2 teaspoons salt
¹/4 teaspoon pepper
¹/2 cup marsala
8 ounces fresh mushrooms, sliced

Cut the veal into 1¹/2-inch pieces. Brown the veal with the onion and garlic in the butter in a skillet. Sprinkle with the flour, salt and pepper and mix well. Cook until bubbly, stirring constantly. Add the wine and cover. Simmer for 15 minutes. Add the mushrooms and simmer for 7 minutes longer.

Serves 4

Risotto Piedmontaise

2¹/2 cups chicken broth
1 small onion, finely chopped
¹/4 cup (¹/2 stick) butter
1 cup uncooked rice
¹/2 teaspoon salt, or to taste
Grated Parmesan cheese to taste

Bring the broth to a simmer in a saucepan. Sauté the onion in the butter in a saucepan until golden brown. Add the rice and sauté for 10 minutes or until the rice is light brown. Add the broth and salt and mix well. Cover and reduce the heat to low. Simmer for 18 to 20 minutes or until the rice is tender and the liquid is absorbed. Stir in Parmesan cheese or sprinkle the cheese over the rice to serve.

Serves 4

Blueberry Muffins La Posada

2 cups all-purpose flour
4 teaspoons baking powder
¹/2 teaspoon salt
¹/3 cup shortening
²/3 cup sugar
2 eggs, beaten
²/3 cup milk
1 cup frozen blueberries, thawed and drained

Preheat the oven to 400 degrees. Sift the flour, baking powder and salt together. Cream the shortening and sugar in a mixing bowl until light and fluffy. Beat in the eggs. Add the sifted flour mixture alternately with the milk, mixing just until combined after each addition. Fold in the blueberries.
Spoon into greased muffin cups, filling one-half full. Bake for 15 minutes. Serve warm or cool on a wire rack.

Makes 1¹/2 dozen

Brandy Flip Pie

1 envelope unflavored gelatin
1/4 cup cold water
4 egg yolks, beaten
1/2 cup milk, scalded
1/4 cup sugar
4 egg whites
1/2 teaspoon ground nutmeg
3 to 4 tablespoons brandy
1/4 cup sugar
1 baked (9-inch) pie shell

Sprinkle the gelatin over the cold water in a cup and let stand to soften. Combine the egg yolks with the milk and 1/4 cup sugar in a double boiler. Cook over simmering water until the mixture coats the back of a spoon. Remove from the heat and add the gelatin mixture, stirring to dissolve completely. Chill until slightly thickened.

Beat the egg whites with the nutmeg, brandy and 1/4 cup sugar in a mixing bowl until stiff peaks form. Fold into the chilled mixture. Spoon into the cooled pie shell. Chill until firm. Serve with whipped cream and garnish with chocolate curls.

Note: Make chocolate curls by shaving slightly warmed bittersweet chocolate or semisweet chocolate with a vegetable peeler.

Serves 6 to 8

CAMELBACK INN,
A JW MARRIOTT RESORT & SPA
"In All the World, Only One"

Jack Stewart conceived the idea, selected the location and named the inn during the early 1930s. He believed the north side of Camelback Mountain was the most scenic and beautiful, and shared his ideas with Edward Loomis Bowes who is credited as "architect/designer."

Stewart and Bowes discussed building a southwestern resort with walls of rounded adobe brick. Stewart wanted horseback riding and other activities in a refined and gracious atmosphere that would attract the well-to-do.

John C. Lincoln owned the original 420 acres between Camelback and Mummy Mountains, and agreed to invest $50,000. Pessimistic expectations were voiced from Phoenix, twelve dusty miles west of the proposed building site: "a mistake," "poor location," "too far from things," "quite a gamble." O'Malley Lumber Company supplied all the lumber and Mr. O'Malley was one of the original investors. The adobe bricks used in constructing the original buildings were made on-site. A rented mule was harnessed to a homemade device that mixed earth, water and straw. This slimy concoction was dropped into wood forms and left to dry in the sun for a week.

The Inn opened in December 1936, with seven casas. There was no swimming pool or bar. Guests trekked across the desert to El Chorro Lodge for cocktails. Stewart, noting the lost revenue, opened the Spanish Cantina bar and a pool in 1938. Also, those who did not want to dress for lunch frequented the table of cold cuts and salads set up, thereby creating the first poolside lunch buffet.

The Marriott family regularly vacationed at Camelback Inn, buying the resort in 1967. The family still visits each spring in March. Wynn Tyner celebrated his 20th year as general manager in December 2005.

SUNDAY BRUNCH

Freshly Squeezed Orange Juice

✦ Kir with Mint

✦ Crunchy French Toast with Maple Syrup

Huevos Rancheros

Crisp Bacon

Jumbo Shrimp with Lemon

✦ Marinated Heirloom Tomatoes in
White Balsamic Vinaigrette

✦ Kahlúa Ice Cream Pie

ROMANTIC DINNER FOR TWO

✦ Lobster Bisque

✦ Spinach Salad with Warm Bacon Dressing

✦ Dover Sole Meunière

Beef Wellington

✦ Chocolate Soufflé with Crème Anglaise

✦ *Recipes Included*

Camelback Inn, a JW Marriot Resort & Spa

Kir with Mint

1 (750-milliliter) bottle of Champagne, chilled
6 sprigs of fresh mint
9 ounces Chambord or black currant juice, chilled

Pour 4 ounces of Champagne into each Champagne glass and add one sprig of mint. Add 1¹/2 ounces of Chambord to each glass and serve immediately.

Serves 6

Crunchy French Toast with Maple Syrup

¹/2 vanilla bean, or 1¹/2 teaspoons vanilla extract
3 eggs
³/4 cup milk
1 teaspoon ground cinnamon
6 (1-inch) slices white bread
2 to 3 cups cornflakes, crushed
6 tablespoons butter
Confectioners' sugar
6 ounces (or more) maple syrup

Split the vanilla bean into halves and scrape the seeds into a medium bowl. Whisk in the eggs, milk and cinnamon. Add the bread and let soak for 1 minute per side. Press each piece of soaked bread into the cornflakes to coat. You may make ahead 1 day in advance up to this point. Wrap in plastic wrap and chill in the refrigerator.

Heat the butter in a skillet over medium heat until the foam subsides. Add the coated bread and cook on each side until brown. Cut each piece into halves and arrange on serving plates. Sprinkle with confectioners' sugar and drizzle with the maple syrup. Serve immediately.

Serves 6

Marinated Heirloom Tomatoes in White Balsamic Vinaigrette

1/2 cup white balsamic vinegar
1/4 cup packed light brown sugar
1 cup extra-virgin olive oil
3 garlic cloves, thinly sliced
3 shallots, thinly sliced

1/4 cup fresh basil leaves, torn
Kosher salt to taste
Freshly ground pepper to taste
5 heirloom tomatoes, cut into wedges

Mix the vinegar and brown sugar in a bowl. Let stand until the brown sugar is completely dissolved. Whisk in the olive oil, garlic, shallots and basil. Season with kosher salt and pepper. Add the tomato wedges and toss gently to coat. Chill for 4 hours before serving. Serve using a slotted spoon.

Serves 6

Kahlúa Ice Cream Pie

4 ounces chocolate chips
1 1/4 tablespoons butter
1/4 teaspoon vanilla extract
1 1/4 cups crisp rice cereal
3/4 cup sliced almonds, toasted
1 pint vanilla ice cream

Kahlúa or coffee-flavored liqueur
    to taste
1/2 cup heavy whipping cream
1/2 teaspoon vanilla extract
1 tablespoon confectioners' sugar
Chocolate candy bar

Melt the chocolate chips and butter in a double boiler over steaming water, stirring until smooth. Stir in 1/4 teaspoon vanilla. Add the cereal and almonds and stir until coated. Press over the bottom and up the side of a 9-inch pie plate. Chill in the freezer.

Beat the ice cream in a bowl of a stand mixer using the paddle attachment until softened. Stir in the Kahlúa and spread in the chilled pie shell. Whip the whipping cream with 1/2 teaspoon vanilla and the confectioners' sugar in a bowl of a stand mixer until soft peaks form. Spread over the ice cream. Scrape a vegetable peeler over the candy bar to make chocolate curls. Sprinkle the chocolate curls over the whipped cream. Serve immediately or store in the freezer.

Note: You may substitute chocolate mint ice cream for the vanilla ice cream, or use layers of vanilla, chocolate and strawberry ice cream instead of using just vanilla ice cream.

Serves 6 to 8

Lobster Bisque

8 ounces yellow onions, chopped
1 teaspoon minced garlic
2 carrots, sliced
1 rib celery, sliced
1/2 fennel bulb
1/3 cup tomato paste (6 ounces)
1 tablespoon sugar
1 bay leaf
2 sprigs of fresh thyme
1/4 bunch fresh parsley
1 teaspoon peppercorns
1/4 cup (1/2 stick) butter
1/4 cup all-purpose flour
1/4 cup Pernod

1/4 cup brandy
1/4 cup white wine
2 cups heavy cream
1/2 gallon Lobster Stock (page 69)
Salt and pepper to taste
1 egg
3 tablespoons water
1 1/4 pounds lobster tail meat,
  cut into pieces
Puff pastry
6 ounces crème fraîche
6 ounces caviar

Sauté the onions, garlic, carrots, celery and fennel in a stockpot until brown. Stir in the tomato paste, sugar, bay leaf, thyme, parsley and peppercorns. Add the butter and cook until melted. Add the flour and stir to mix well. Add the Pernod, brandy and white wine. Cook until the mixture is reduced to a glaze, stirring to deglaze the stockpot. Add the cream and lobster stock. Simmer until the mixture coats a spoon. Strain through a chinois or fine mesh sieve into a bowl, discarding the solids. Season with salt and pepper to taste.

To serve, preheat the oven to 400 degrees. Beat the egg and water in a bowl. Place 2 to 4 ounces of the lobster meat into each ovenproof soup bowl. Ladle 6 ounces of the bisque into each bowl. Cut a piece of the puff pastry big enough to cover the top of each bowl. Score the pastry with the tip of a knife. Brush the rim of the bowls and the edges under the pastry with some of the egg mixture. Lay the pastry over the bowls and press firmly to seal. Brush the pastry tops with the remaining egg mixture. Bake for 8 minutes or until the pastry rises about 2 inches. Poke a hole in each pastry and spoon in the crème fraîche and caviar.

Note: Pernod is an anise-based, licorice-flavored French aperitif. Purchased fish glace can be used in place of the lobster stock, using the package directions.

Serves 8 to 10

Lobster Stock

10 pounds lobster shells
1/3 cup tomato paste
4 garlic cloves, chopped
1 pound yellow onions, chopped
4 large carrots, chopped
4 ribs celery, chopped
1 cup red wine
1 bay leaf
2 sprigs fresh thyme
1/4 bunch fresh parsley
1 teaspoon peppercorns
3 gallons water

Preheat the oven to 350 degrees. Place the lobster shells in a single layer on a rimmed baking sheet. Bake for 20 minutes. Remove from the oven and spread the tomato paste over the shells. Bake for 10 to 15 minutes or until the tomato paste is caramelized. Sauté the garlic, onions, carrots and celery in a stockpot until brown. Add the red wine. Cook until the mixture is reduced by half, stirring to deglaze the stockpot. Add the bay leaf, thyme, parsley, peppercorns, roasted shell mixture and water and bring to a simmer. Simmer for 2 hours. Strain the mixture into a large container, discarding the solids. Chill in the refrigerator until ready to use.

Makes 1 gallon

Spinach Salad with Warm Bacon Dressing

4 ounces bacon, chopped and cooked
1/4 cup Warm Bacon Dressing (below)
1 pound baby spinach
4 ounces goat cheese
1 Bartlett pear, sliced

Slightly heat the bacon and dressing in a sauté pan. Pour over the spinach in a salad bowl and toss to coat. Crumble the goat cheese over the spinach mixture and top with the pear slices.

Serves 4

Warm Bacon Dressing

1¹/2 pounds peppered bacon, chopped
¹/2 cup rice wine vinegar
2 teaspoons Dijon mustard
1 teaspoon whole grain mustard
Sugar to taste
Salt and pepper to taste

Cook the bacon in a skillet until crisp. Remove the bacon to paper towels to drain and reserve for another purpose. Drain the bacon drippings from the skillet, reserving ³/4 cup. Mix the vinegar, Dijon mustard and whole grain mustard in a bowl. Heat the reserved bacon drippings in a saucepan until slightly warm. Whisk into the mustard mixture. Add the sugar, salt and pepper and mix well.

Makes 1¹/4 cups

Dover Sole Meunière

1/4 cup all-purpose flour
Salt and pepper to taste
1 whole Dover sole, cleaned, skinned
    and fin bones removed
2 tablespoons olive oil
1/2 lemon

3 tablespoons butter, softened
6 ounces baby spinach
1 garlic clove, roasted
2 teaspoons olive oil
Beurre Meunière (below)

Preheat the oven to 350 degrees. Mix the flour, salt and pepper in a shallow dish. Dredge the fish in the flour mixture to coat. Heat 2 tablespoons olive oil in an ovenproof sauté pan. Place the fish in the prepared pan and squeeze the lemon over the fish. Cook for 2 to 3 minutes per side or until brown. Place the butter on top of the fish. Bake for 6 to 10 minutes or until the fish flakes easily. Remove from the oven and let stand for a couple of minutes. Separate the top fillet from the bone from the head down to the tail using a fish spatula. Repeat the process removing the backbone from the bottom fillet. Place the bottom fillet on a serving plate and place the top fillet off center over the bottom fillet.

Sauté the spinach and roasted garlic in 2 teaspoons olive oil in a sauté pan until wilted. Arrange around the fish. Serve with beurre meunière.

Serves 1

Beurre Meunière

1 pound (4 sticks) butter
1 1/2 teaspoons parsley, chopped
Juice of 1 lemon

Melt the butter in a small saucepan and bring to a boil. Reduce the heat and simmer for 5 minutes. Some of the milk solids will rise to the top and some will collect on the bottom of the pan. Skim the solids from the surface. Pour the clarified butter slowly off the top, leaving the white milk solids in the bottom of the pan. Continue to cook until the solids are a dark brown and have an almond-like flavor. Strain through a chinois or fine-mesh sieve into a bowl. Stir in the parsley and lemon juice.

Note: You may chill the clarified butter until solidified, cut into cubes and store in the refrigerator or freezer.

Makes 1/2 to 1 cup

Chocolate Soufflé with Crème Anglaise

Crème Anglaise
- 1 cup milk
- 1 vanilla bean, split lengthwise, or
   - 1 1/2 teaspoons vanilla extract
- 3 egg yolks
- 1/4 cup sugar

Soufflé
- 1/4 cup (1/2 stick) butter, softened
- 1/2 cup all-purpose flour
- 1 cup milk
- 2 ounces semisweet chocolate
- 2 tablespoons baking cocoa, sifted
- 1 teaspoon vanilla extract
- 1 egg white
- 4 egg yolks
- 4 egg whites
- 6 tablespoons sugar

For the crème anglaise, bring the milk and vanilla bean to a boil in a saucepan over high heat. Remove from the heat and let stand, covered, for 15 minutes to infuse the flavor. Whisk the egg yolks and sugar in a mixing bowl until thick and pale yellow. Bring the milk mixture to a simmer. Pour a little of the simmering milk into the egg yolk mixture, whisking constantly. Return to the milk in the saucepan, stirring constantly. Cook over low heat for 1 minute or until thickened, stirring constantly with a wooden spoon. Do not boil. To test for doneness, run your finger down the back of the spoon. If sufficiently cooked, the mark will hold. The sauce should be the consistency of thick cream. Strain the sauce through a fine-mesh sieve into a chilled bowl and stir occasionally. Cover and chill in the refrigerator. The sauce may be made up to 1 day in advance.

For the soufflé, preheat the oven to 400 degrees. Cut the butter into the flour in a bowl until crumbly. Shape into a ball and then break into small pieces. Bring the milk, chocolate and baking cocoa to a boil in a saucepan. Stir in the flour mixture. Remove from the heat. Whisk in the vanilla and one egg white. Spoon into a bowl and let cool to lukewarm. Stir in the egg yolks one at a time. Whip four egg whites in a mixing bowl. Add the sugar gradually, beating until soft peaks form. Fold into the chocolate mixture. Spoon into six 4-ounce soufflé dishes. Bake for 30 minutes or until puffed.

To serve, break the top of each soufflé and add the crème anglaise.

Serves 6

EL CHORRO LODGE

Paradise Valley's "Cheers—Where Everybody Knows Your Name"

John C. Lincoln built the structure in 1934 to house the Judson School for Girls where his daughter, Lillian, attended. Today, the El Chorro bar is the original schoolroom.

In 1937, Jan and Mark Gruber bought the property and turned it into a lodge and dining room. Guests of the newly opened Camelback Inn next door, where no adult beverages were available, quickly wore a path to the welcoming El Chorro. Drinks were 25 cents and dinners were $1.50 to $1.75. Hollywood celebrities of the 1930s loved the mesquite fireplace on the outdoor patio (still welcoming guests today) and the sweet smell of the world-famous sticky buns, a Gruber family recipe.

A 21-year-old bartender named Joe Miller was hired in 1952. Buzz Dublin, owner of Lulu Belle's, another Scottsdale landmark, told Joe about a newly hired cocktail waitress— Evie Awbery, a Montana girl, who came to the Valley from Seattle. Joe thought she was really cute and she thought he was a "high-flyin' big man from a big city." And, "the rest is history."

The Millers bought El Chorro from Mark Gruber in 1952 after Jan died. Today, this Paradise Valley restaurant is open year round, with a loyal group of locals regularly stopping by. Evie once said, "Locals come first, trumping tourists." Regular patrons see El Chorro as sort of their own private club.

Locals and tourists enjoy chicken livers with a rasher of bacon or shad roe on toast from the luncheon menu along with a scrumptious rack of lamb and, always, sticky buns at dinnertime.

LUNCHEON MENU

- ◆ Spicy Rustic Tomato Soup
- ◆ Curried Chicken Salad with Curried Mayonnaise Sauce
- ◆ El Chorro Lodge Famous Sticky Buns
- ◆ Chocolate Icebox Cake

DINNER MENU

- ◆ Black Bean and Salsa Soup
- ◆ Dungeness Crab Cakes with Rémoulade Sauce
- ◆ Spring Field Greens with Raspberry Vinaigrette
- ◆ Mesquite-Grilled Filet Mignon with Shallot Butter
- ◆ Roasted Garlic Mashed Potatoes
- ◆ Caramel Custard Flan

- ◆ *Recipes Included*

El Chorro Lodge

Spicy Rustic Tomato Soup

1/2 cup (3/8-inch) chopped onion
2 tablespoons minced shallot
1 tablespoon minced garlic
1/4 teaspoon crushed red pepper flakes, or to taste
2 tablespoons olive oil
1 tablespoon dried basil
1 tablespoon ground cumin
1 tablespoon kosher salt
1 1/2 cups canned diced tomatoes with juice
1 cup canned crushed tomatoes
1/4 cup tomato paste
1/2 cup vegetable juice cocktail
1 quart chicken stock
1/4 cup orange juice
Grated zest and juice of 1 orange
1/4 cup packed coarsely chopped fresh basil
Sour cream
1/4 cup fresh parsley, finely chopped

Sauté the onion, shallot, garlic and crushed red pepper flakes in the olive oil in a large stockpot over medium heat until the onion is translucent. Add the dried basil and cumin and sauté for 1 minute. Add the kosher salt, undrained diced tomatoes, crushed tomatoes, tomato paste, vegetable juice cocktail, stock and 1/4 cup orange juice. Bring to a gentle boil and reduce the heat. Simmer for 45 minutes, stirring frequently. Remove from the heat. Stir in the orange zest, fresh basil and freshly squeezed orange juice. Ladle into soup bowls. Top each serving with a dollop of sour cream and some of the parsley.

Makes 1 1/2 quarts

Curried Chicken Salad with Curried Mayonnaise Sauce

3 pounds boneless skinless
    chicken breasts
2 quarts water
1 tablespoon kosher salt
2 tablespoons curry powder
Curried Mayonnaise Sauce (below)
1 head green leaf lettuce, separated
    into leaves

$2^{1}/4$ quarts spring mix salad greens
$3/4$ cup mango chutney
$1/2$ cup shredded coconut, toasted
1 cantaloupe, peeled and sliced
1 honeydew melon, peeled and sliced
1 pineapple, peeled and sliced
12 strawberries, sliced

Bring the chicken, water, kosher salt and curry powder to a boil in a saucepan. Reduce the heat and simmer for 30 minutes or until the chicken is tender; drain. Cut the chicken into $1/2$-inch pieces into a bowl. Add enough of the curry mayonnaise sauce to bind together. Cover and chill for 2 hours or longer before serving.

To serve, line each salad plate with green leaf lettuce. Place $1^{1}/2$ cups of the spring mix salad greens in the center. Spoon $1/2$ cup of the chicken salad on the salad greens and top with 1 to 2 tablespoons mango chutney. Sprinkle with the toasted coconut. Arrange the sliced fruit on each plate.

Serves 6

Curried Mayonnaise Sauce

2 tablespoons minced celery
2 tablespoons minced yellow onion
$1/4$ cup finely chopped dried apricots
2 tablespoons finely chopped raisins
$1^{1}/2$ cups mayonnaise
2 tablespoons curry powder
$1/2$ teaspoon kosher salt

$1/4$ teaspoon white pepper
1 tablespoon white wine
1 tablespoon fresh lemon juice
Dash of Tabasco sauce
$1/2$ teaspoon Worcestershire sauce
2 tablespoons apricot nectar
2 tablespoons mango chutney

Combine the celery, onion, apricots, raisins, mayonnaise, curry powder, kosher salt, white pepper, wine, lemon juice, Tabasco sauce, Worcestershire sauce, apricot nectar and mango chutney in a bowl and mix well. Chill, covered, for 2 hours or longer before using.

Makes 1 pint

El Chorro Lodge Famous Sticky Buns

2 envelopes dry yeast
1/3 cup warm
    (105 to 115 degrees) water
1 2/3 cups warm
    (105 to 115 degrees) milk
3 tablespoons shortening or
    unsalted butter
3 tablespoons granulated sugar
2 teaspoons salt
5 cups all-purpose flour

1/4 cup water
3 tablespoons ground cinnamon
1 1/2 cups packed light brown sugar
1/2 cup (1 stick) butter, softened
2 cups packed light brown sugar
1 cup (2 sticks) butter, softened
1/2 cup light corn syrup
2 tablespoons water
1/4 cup water

Dissolve the yeast in 1/3 cup warm water in a bowl. Combine the warm milk, shortening, granulated sugar and salt in a large mixing bowl. Stir in the yeast mixture. Add 2 cups of the flour and stir until well blended. Continue adding enough of the remaining flour to form a soft dough. Place the dough on a lightly floured surface and knead gently for 1 minute to form a smooth ball. Place in a lightly greased large bowl, turning to coat the surface. Cover and let rise in a warm place for 30 to 40 minutes or until doubled in bulk.

Combine 1/4 cup water and the cinnamon in a bowl and mix until smooth. Add 1 1/2 cups brown sugar and 1/2 cup butter and beat until smooth to form a cinnamon smear.

Combine 2 cups brown sugar, 1 cup butter, the corn syrup and 2 tablespoons water in a bowl and beat until smooth to form a caramel smear.

Place the dough on a lightly floured surface and divide into two equal portions. Invert a bowl over one portion. Roll the remaining portion into a 9×18-inch rectangle. Spread half of the cinnamon smear evenly over the dough and roll up to enclose the filling, pinching to seal the seam. Cut into 1 1/2-inch pieces. Repeat with the remaining dough and cinnamon smear.

Spread half the caramel smear in a 9×13-inch baking pan and arrange the rolls in a single layer in the pan. Spread the top of the rolls with the remaining caramel smear. Let rise for 30 minutes or until doubled in bulk.

Preheat the oven to 325 degrees. Sprinkle 1/4 cup water evenly over the rolls and place on the middle oven rack. Place a large foil-lined baking sheet directly under the pan to catch any drips. Bake for 10 to 12 minutes and gently press the rolls down with a metal spatula. Bake for 15 to 20 minutes longer or until golden brown. Remove from the oven and cool for 5 minutes. Invert onto a large heat-proof dish or baking sheet.

Serves 15

Chocolate Icebox Cake

2 cups graham cracker crumbs
3 tablespoons granulated sugar
1/4 cup (1/2 stick) butter, melted
1 3/4 pounds semisweet chocolate
7 cups heavy whipping cream
2 ounces (1/2 cup) confectioners' sugar
7 egg whites
2/3 cup granulated sugar
1 teaspoon cream of tartar
1 1/2 tablespoons unflavored gelatin
1/3 cup hot water
1 cup chopped walnuts, lightly toasted

Preheat the oven to 350 degrees. Process the graham cracker crumbs, 3 tablespoons granulated sugar and the butter in a food processor until combined. Press over the bottom of a 9×13-inch baking pan. Bake for 10 to 12 minutes or until golden brown. Remove from the oven to cool.

Melt the chocolate in a double boiler over simmering water and keep warm. Whip the cream with the confectioners' sugar in a mixing bowl until stiff peaks form. Whip the egg whites, 2/3 cup granulated sugar and the cream of tartar in a mixing bowl until stiff peaks form. Fold in the melted chocolate. Add half the whipped cream mixture and mix until thoroughly incorporated. Dissolve the gelatin in the hot water. Add to the remaining whipped cream mixture. Fold into the chocolate mixture. Pour into the cooled crust and sprinkle with the walnuts. Freeze, uncovered, for 8 to 10 hours. Cover with plastic wrap and freeze until ready to serve.

Serves 15

Black Bean and Salsa Soup

2 cups dried black beans
1¹/2 quarts water
2 cups vegetable juice cocktail
1 tablespoon granulated garlic
1 tablespoon ground cumin
¹/4 teaspoon crushed red pepper
1 tablespoon kosher salt
2 tablespoons all-purpose flour
1 tablespoon olive oil
2 cups salsa
1 cup sour cream, stirred
¹/2 cup finely chopped green onions
¹/2 cup salsa

Sort and rinse the beans. Place in a bowl and add enough cold water to cover twice the volume of the beans. Chill in the refrigerator for 8 to 10 hours.

Drain the beans. Combine the beans, 1¹/2 quarts water, the vegetable juice cocktail, garlic, cumin, red pepper and kosher salt in a large stockpot and mix well. Bring to a boil over medium heat. Reduce the heat to low and simmer for 3 to 4 hours or until the beans are tender, stirring frequently and adding additional water if needed. Blend the flour and olive oil in a small bowl to form a smooth paste. Stir into the soup. Stir in 2 cups salsa. Simmer for 30 minutes. Adjust the seasonings to taste. Ladle into soup bowls and top with sour cream, green onions and ¹/2 cup salsa.

Note: You may use 3 cups drained, rinsed canned black beans and simmer for 1 to 1¹/2 hours.

Makes 1¹/2 quarts

Dungeness Crab Cakes with Rémoulade Sauce

1/4 cup minced yellow onion
1/4 cup minced celery
2 tablespoons minced red bell pepper
2 tablespoons minced yellow
   bell pepper
1 tablespoon minced garlic
2 tablespoons olive oil
2 eggs
1/4 cup mayonnaise
2 tablespoons sour cream

2 tablespoons Worcestershire sauce
2 tablespoons minced parsley
2 tablespoons Old Bay seasoning
2 cups panko (Japanese bread crumbs)
2 1/2 pounds Dungeness crab meat,
   drained and flaked
3/4 cup dry bread crumbs
2 tablespoons butter, clarified
2 tablespoons olive oil
Rémoulade Sauce (below)

Sauté the onion, celery, bell peppers and garlic in 2 tablespoons olive oil in a skillet for 3 to 5 minutes or until tender-crisp; do not brown. Remove from the heat to cool. Whisk the eggs, mayonnaise, sour cream, Worcestershire sauce, parsley and Old Bay seasoning in a large bowl. Add the cooled vegetables and mix well. Fold in the panko and crab meat. Divide into sixteen equal portions and shape into patties. Chill for 2 hours. Coat the patties lightly with the dry bread crumbs. Sauté the patties in a mixture of the clarified butter and 2 tablespoons olive oil in a large skillet until golden brown, turning once and adding additional olive oil if needed. Serve with the Rémoulade Sauce.

Serves 8

Rémoulade Sauce

1/4 cup coarsely chopped yellow onion
1/4 cup coarsely chopped dill pickle
1 tablespoon coarsely chopped
   fresh parsley
2 cups mayonnaise

2 tablespoons Dijon mustard
2 tablespoons bottled chili sauce
2 tablespoons horseradish
1/2 teaspoon dried tarragon
1 1/2 teaspoons fresh lemon juice

Process the onion, dill pickle and parsley in a food processor; drain. Combine with the mayonnaise in a bowl. Stir in the Dijon mustard, chili sauce, horseradish, tarragon and lemon juice. Chill for 4 hours or longer before serving.

Makes 2 1/2 cups

Raspberry Vinaigrette

3/4 cup raspberry fruit spread
3/4 cup canola oil or walnut oil, or a combination
1/3 cup red raspberry wine vinegar
Kosher salt and pepper to taste

Place the raspberry fruit spread in a food processor container. Add the canola oil and vinegar alternately, processing constantly. Season with kosher salt and pepper. Pour into a covered container. Chill, covered, for 4 hours or longer before serving.

Makes 1 pint

Mesquite-Grilled Filet Mignon with Shallot Butter

3 shallots, minced
2 garlic cloves, minced
1/4 cup extra-virgin olive oil
1/4 cup (1/2 stick) butter, clarified and melted
6 (8-ounce) filets mignons
Salt and pepper to taste

Sauté the shallots and garlic in the olive oil in a skillet until tender; do not brown. Add the clarified butter and simmer gently for 5 minutes. Preheat the grill using mesquite charcoal. Place the filets mignons on a grill rack and grill to the desired degree of doneness. Season with salt and pepper. Place on serving plates and brush with the shallot butter. You may also preheat the broiler and broil the filets mignons on a rack in a broiler pan.

Serves 6

Roasted Garlic Mashed Potatoes

3 garlic heads
1/4 cup extra-virgin olive oil
1 tablespoon dried thyme
6 (8- to 10-ounce) russet potatoes
Salt to taste
1/4 cup milk
3/4 cup buttermilk
1/4 cup (1/2 stick) unsalted butter
Pepper to taste

Preheat the oven to 350 degrees. Peel the garlic, leaving the cloves whole, or use the whole heads. Place in a shallow baking dish and drizzle with the olive oil to coat. Sprinkle with the thyme. Bake, covered, for 30 minutes or until tender and golden brown. Drain, reserving the olive oil for another use.

Peel the potatoes and cut into quarters. Bring the potatoes to a boil in salted water to cover in a saucepan and reduce the heat. Simmer for 20 minutes or until tender. Heat the milk, buttermilk and butter in a saucepan. Do not boil. Drain the potatoes and return to the saucepan. Squeeze the garlic out of the heads into the potatoes. Add the milk mixture gradually, beating constantly until smooth and of the desired consistency. Season with salt and pepper.

Serves 8

Caramel Custard Flan

2 to 3 cups sugar
3 1/4 cups milk
1 3/4 cups heavy cream
1 cup sugar
5 extra-large eggs
5 egg yolks
2 tablespoons rum
1 teaspoon vanilla extract

Preheat the oven to 300 degrees. Heat a sauté pan over medium heat. Add 2 to 3 cups sugar gradually, making sure that each addition of sugar is melted before adding more. Heat until all of the sugar is melted and light brown. Pour evenly into eight custard cups to just cover the bottom. Place the custard cups in a 9×13-inch baking pan.

Scald the milk, cream and 1 cup sugar in a heavy saucepan. Combine the eggs, egg yolks, rum and vanilla in a large bowl and mix well. Whisk the scalded milk mixture into the egg mixture gradually until smooth. Pour into the prepared custard cups, filling to the top. Add enough water to the larger pan to come two-thirds of the way from the top of the cups. Bake for 1 hour or until the tops are firm. Remove from the pan and cool on a wire rack. Loosen the flan from the side of each cup with a knife. Invert onto a serving plate and garnish with whipped cream and fresh strawberries.

Serves 8

FOUR PEAKS BREWING COMPANY
"Don't Forget Your Growler to Go"

Four Peaks Brewing Company resides in the old Borden's Creamery building, built before the turn of the century in 1892, on 8th Street in Tempe. An excellent architectural example of original Mission Revival style and constructed mostly of old brick, the building has wooden ceilings and a 35-foot-high glass clerestory that is supported by steel suspension. No additions were added after 1927, and the building's design set the character for the surrounding neighborhood.

Four Peaks Brewing Company opened its doors ten years ago with only handcrafted ales. Master Brewer Andy Ingram offers up to ten different styles of beer on tap, including two cask-conditioned ales drawn with authentic beer engines. Keg and bottled beers are delivered to local restaurants, bars, resorts and liquor stores.

With a yearly production capacity of 10,000 barrels of beer (20,000 kegs), Four Peaks uses reverse osmosis to strip its water of contaminants. By adding certain chemicals, the brewery can emulate some of the great brewing waters of Europe. For example, they use Burton water, a very hard water from the middle of England, for their 8th Street Ale and IPA. Four Peaks' notable brands are Kiltlifter, 8th Street Ale, Hefeweizen and Hop Knot IPA. Customers can choose half-gallon growlers to go; these are containers used to carry beer from a pub or brewery.

The kitchen provides an excellent selection of original pub fare, sandwiches and plated entrées that include fish and chips, carne adovada, pizza and "Old Creamery" desserts for lunch and dinner. Try an Oatmeal Stout Shake made with vanilla bean ice cream and oatmeal stout. Open every day from 11 a.m. to 2 a.m., with happy hour from 3 p.m. to 7 p.m.

LUNCHEON MENU

Vine-Ripened Tomatoes with Grilled Onions
and Blue Cheese Dressing

◆ Mixed Greens with Pineapple Hoisin Vinaigrette

◆ Halibut with Penne and Basil Pesto

Crème Brûlée with Seasonal Berries

BEER DINNER MENU

Wild Game Chili

Hopknot Beer

◆ Duck Cakes with Spicy Nopales Salsa

Fool's Gold Beer

◆ Lamb Braciole

Kiltlifter Beer

◆ Buffalo Spring Rolls with Plum Dressing

8th Street Ale

◆ Stout Shake

◆ *Recipes Included*

Four Peaks Brewing Company

Pineapple Hoisin Vinaigrette

2/3 cup pineapple juice
2 green onions, sliced 1/4 inch thick
1 teaspoon minced fresh cilantro
3 tablespoons hoisin sauce
1/2 teaspoon crushed red pepper
1 tablespoon minced fresh ginger
1 teaspoon minced garlic
1 tablespoon rice vinegar or lemon juice
2 tablespoons sesame oil
3 tablespoons canola oil

Process the pineapple juice, green onions, cilantro, hoisin sauce, red pepper, ginger, garlic and vinegar in a blender. Add the sesame oil and canola oil in a fine stream, processing constantly. Chill until ready to use. Serve over mixed salad greens topped with chopped red bell peppers, black sesame seeds, mandarin oranges or toasted almonds or a combination.

Note: Hoisin sauce is a thick, reddish-brown, sweet-and-spicy sauce made from soybeans, garlic, chiles and various spices. It can be purchased in most grocery stores or Asian markets.

Makes about 1 1/2 cups

Halibut with Penne and Basil Pesto

4 (4-ounce) halibut fillets
Salt and pepper to taste
3 tablespoons olive oil
2 cups heavy cream
1/2 cup Basil Pesto (below)
1 pound penne, cooked and drained
1 cup chopped Roma tomatoes

Season the fish with salt and pepper. Cook the fish in the olive oil in a sauté pan for 2 minutes per side or until medium done. Keep warm. Bring the cream to a boil in a large saucepan and cook until slightly reduced. Stir in the pesto. Add the pasta. Heat until the pasta is coated evenly, stirring constantly. Cut the fish into 1-inch cubes. Divide the pasta among four serving plates. Top with the fish and sprinkle with the tomatoes.

Serves 4

Basil Pesto

1 cup fresh basil leaves, tightly packed
1 tablespoon pine nuts, toasted
2 tablespoons olive oil
1 garlic clove
Salt and pepper to taste
2 teaspoons freshly grated Parmesan cheese

Pulse the basil leaves, pine nuts, olive oil, garlic, salt and pepper in a blender until coarsely chopped. Add the cheese and pulse a few more times until blended.

Makes 1/2 cup

Duck Cakes with Spicy Nopales Salsa

Spicy Nopales Salsa
1/4 cup finely chopped fresh nopales cactus pads
3 serrano chiles, finely chopped, or to taste
3 tomatoes, chopped
1/4 cup fresh cilantro, chopped
4 green onions, white part only, chopped
Juice of 2 limes

Duck Cakes
2 duck breasts, cooked and shredded
1 red bell pepper, finely chopped
1 yellow bell pepper, finely chopped
1/4 cup fresh cilantro, chopped
1/4 cup roasted corn kernels
4 eggs, beaten
1/2 cup bread crumbs
3 to 4 teaspoons canola oil

For the salsa, combine the cactus, chiles, tomatoes, cilantro, green onions and lime juice in a bowl and mix well.

For the duck cakes, combine the duck, bell peppers, cilantro, corn and eggs in a bowl and mix well. Shape into 3 1/2-inch cakes and sprinkle evenly with the bread crumbs. Fry in the canola oil in a skillet over medium-high heat for 1 1/2 minutes per side. Serve over the salsa.

Note: The duck breasts can be purchased at Asian markets.

Serves 4

Lamb Braciole

Gremolata
>   Grated zest of 1 lemon
>   2 garlic cloves, minced
>   2 tablespoons chopped fresh Italian parsley

Lamb
>   2 pounds lamb round
>   1¹/2 cups (12 ounces) ground lamb
>   6 purple potatoes, chopped
>   2 garlic cloves, minced
>   1 tablespoon chopped fresh basil
>   1 tablespoon chopped fresh oregano
>   Salt and freshly ground pepper to taste
>   ³/4 cup mirepoix (25 percent carrots, 50 percent onions and
>   25 percent celery by weight)
>   1 bottle of Kiltlifter or other dark beer
>   3 cups lamb stock, or to cover
>   1 pound orecchiette or other small pasta, cooked and drained

For the gremolata, combine the lemon zest, garlic and parsley in a bowl and toss to mix well.

For the lamb, preheat the oven to 350 degrees. Cut the lamb round into six pieces and pound until thin. Spread each with the ground lamb, potatoes, garlic, basil, oregano, salt and pepper and roll up to enclose the filling. Place the mirepoix in an ovenproof stockpot. Stack the lamb roll-ups on the mirepoix. Bake for 25 minutes. Reduce the oven temperature to 300 degrees. Pour the beer and lamb stock over the roll-ups to cover. Cover and bake for 1 to 1¹/2 hours. Remove the lamb roll-ups from the liquid and cut on the bias into slices. Cook the liquid until reduced to a sauce consistency.

To serve, place the lamb on top of the cooked pasta and drizzle with the thickened sauce. Sprinkle with the gremolata.

Note: You may use lamb glace for the lamb stock, or make your own stock using lamb bones.

Serves 6

Buffalo Spring Rolls with Plum Dressing

Plum Dressing
   3/4 cup prepared plum sauce
   2 tablespoons rice vinegar
   3 green onions, white part only

Spring Rolls
   1 cup ground buffalo
   1 jalapeño chile, chopped

1 cup shredded napa cabbage
3/4 cup finely chopped daikon radish
1 cup fresh corn kernels
1/4 cup chopped fresh cilantro
8 spring roll wrappers
Egg wash
Vegetable oil for deep-frying
1 pound mixed baby greens

For the dressing, whisk the plum sauce, rice vinegar and green onions in a bowl.

For the spring rolls, brown the ground buffalo in a skillet, stirring until crumbly. Add the jalapeño chile, napa cabbage, daikon radish, corn and cilantro and mix well. Simmer for 5 to 7 minutes or until tender. Remove from the heat and cool slightly. Spoon the buffalo mixture into the spring roll wrappers and roll up as for burritos, brushing the edges with egg wash to seal. Preheat the oil to 350 degrees in a deep fryer. Deep-fry the spring rolls for 2 minutes; drain.

To serve, coat the mixed baby greens with the dressing and divide evenly among eight serving plates. Top each serving with one spring roll.

Note: Egg wash is a mixture of beaten eggs and a liquid used to glue the wrapper together or to coat dough before baking to add sheen.

Serves 8

Stout Shake

   1 1/2 cups vanilla bean ice cream
   1/4 cup oatmeal stout beer

Process the ice cream and beer in a blender until smooth. Pour into two serving glasses. Garnish each with chocolate syrup and a dollop of whipped cream.

Serves 2

HERMOSA INN
Los Arcos—Casa Hermosa—Hermosa Inn

Alonzo "Lon" Megargee, Arizona's first recognized Cowboy Artist, was born in Philadelphia and came west at the turn of the last century, earning his keep as bronco buster, cowboy and stud poker dealer; he was also a commercial artist and home builder. He bought the site of the present Hermosa Inn, an isolated plot of land miles from the city limits of Phoenix, because it "spoke" to him. He built his studio of adobe bricks right in the middle of the site and kept adding to it, calling his home Los Arcos and later Casa Hermosa, meaning "beautiful house."

With no formal plans and influenced by the architecture he studied in Spain and Mexico, he used old wooden beams from an abandoned mine and poured a mixture of oil and ash from the roof to age the exterior walls. Because his many guests enjoyed lengthy stays at Casa Hermosa, he began running a guest ranch to supplement his artist's income. The local sheriff was certain there was illegal gambling so the creative Megargee built a tunnel out to the stables for an easy escape into the desert if the law made a surprise visit.

Megargee's noted works include *A Cowboy's Dream*, painted for A-1 Brewery, and a series he painted for Arizona's Capitol Building, commissioned by Governor George W. P. Hunt. His claim to immortality is his painting of a horse drinking from a cowboy's hat entitled *The Last Drop from His Stetson*. This image still graces the inside of every Stetson produced today.

Succeeding owners renamed the property Hermosa Inn, added a pool, tennis courts, casitas and villas. In 1987, a fire severely damaged the main building— Megargee's old home.

Fred and Jennifer Unger bought the Inn in 1992 and have restored the adobe walls, charred beams and ironwork in the fire-damaged main building. Photographs of Megargee and prints of his art grace the walls. The building now houses guest reception, a bar and "Lon's at the Hermosa Inn," a fine dining restaurant recognized not only locally but throughout the U.S. resort world. Inspired by Megargee tales of underground tunnels, the Ungers recently added a subterranean wine room and board room, using recycled bricks, planks, antique hacienda and church doors from Mexico to create a "dramatically different and handsome venue."

LON'S LUNCHEON MENU

◆ Sweet Potato Corn Chowder

◆ Roasted Chicken and Strawberry Salad with
Prickly Pear Vinaigrette

◆ Almond Macaroons

LON'S DINNER MENU

Sea Scallops with Black Truffle Spaetzle

◆ Salmon with Ancho Chile Glaze

◆ Roasted Fingerling Potatoes

◆ Grilled Fennel

◆ Brownie Puddle

◆ *Recipes Included*

Hermosa Inn

Sweet Potato Corn Chowder

1 poblano chile, finely chopped
1 yellow bell pepper, finely chopped
1 red bell pepper, finely chopped
1 tablespoon chopped garlic
2 tablespoons butter

5 ears of corn, roasted and kernels cut
   from the cob
2 large sweet potatoes, finely chopped
1 tablespoon chopped fresh cilantro
Salt and freshly ground pepper to taste

Sweat the poblano chile, bell peppers and garlic in the butter in a saucepan over low heat until tender. Add the corn, sweet potatoes and cilantro. Cover with water and simmer until all of the ingredients are tender. Process half the chowder in a blender until smooth and return to the saucepan. Season with salt and pepper and ladle into soup bowls.

Note: Sweating is cooking a food (typically vegetables) in a small amount of fat, usually covered, over low heat without browning until the food softens and releases moisture; sweating allows the food to release its flavor more quickly when it is later cooked with other foods.

Serves 6 to 8

Roasted Chicken and Strawberry Salad with Prickly Pear Vinaigrette

4 cups pulled roasted chicken
8 ounces fresh mozzarella cheese, chopped
1 cup fresh strawberry quarters
12 cups baby salad greens
Prickly Pear Vinaigrette (page 97)
3 ounces sliced almonds, toasted

Combine the chicken, cheese, strawberries and salad greens in a large salad bowl and toss to mix. Add the vinaigrette and toss to coat. Sprinkle with the toasted almonds.

Serves 6

Prickly Pear Vinaigrette

1/4 cup chopped shallots
2 fresh pears, peeled and
   cut into quarters
1/2 cup olive oil
Olive oil

1/3 cup white balsamic vinegar
1/3 cup prickly pear syrup
2 ice cubes
Salt and pepper to taste

Sweat the shallots and pears in 1/2 cup olive oil in a saucepan for 15 minutes. Remove from the heat to cool. Drain, reserving the cooking liquid. Add enough olive oil to the reserved liquid to measure 1/2 cup. Process the cooked pear mixture, vinegar and prickly pear syrup in a blender until smooth. Add the olive oil mixture gradually, processing constantly until the mixture begins to thicken. Add the ice cubes one at a time, processing constantly until of the desired consistency. Season with salt and pepper.

Note: You may not need to use both of the ice cubes. The ice cubes keep the vinaigrette chilled and help keep the vinaigrette from becoming too thick as it is blended.

Serves 6

Almond Macaroons

4 cups almond paste
2 cups granulated sugar
2 cups confectioners' sugar
1 1/4 cups egg whites

Preheat the oven to 350 degrees. Place the almond paste in a bowl of a stand mixer fitted with a paddle attachment and beat until the paste is broken up. Add the granulated sugar and confectioners' sugar gradually, beating constantly. Shut off the mixer and scrape the side of the bowl to make sure the almond paste is incorporated. Turn the mixer to speed one and add the egg whites in a fine stream. Turn the mixer to speed two and beat for 20 seconds. Spoon the batter into a large cloth piping bag fitted with a 1/4-inch plain tip. Pipe the batter in rows onto cookie sheets lined with baking parchment paper, allowing 1 inch around each cookie. Tap the cookies with a damp towel to give them their signature crackle. Bake for 12 to 15 minutes or until light golden brown. Cool on the cookie sheets.

Note: These cookies may be stored in the freezer for 1 week, but are best enjoyed the day they are made.

Makes 2 to 3 dozen

Salmon with Ancho Chile Glaze

Tarragon Tomato Sauce
  2 Roma tomatoes, cored
  Olive oil
  1 cup chicken stock
  1 tablespoon chopped fresh tarragon
  1/4 cup extra-virgin olive oil
  Salt and pepper to taste

Salmon
  1 teaspoon lemon juice
  1 teaspoon ancho chile flakes
  1/2 cup honey
  4 (6-ounce) wild salmon fillets
  Vegetable oil
  Salt and pepper to taste
  Roasted Fingerling Potatoes
    (page 100)
  Grilled Fennel (page 100)

For the sauce, preheat the oven or grill to 325 degrees. Brush the tomatoes with olive oil and place in a baking pan or on a grill rack. Bake or grill for 30 to 45 minutes or until roasted. Remove from the oven or grill to cool. Peel the tomatoes. Cut into halves and squeeze out the seeds. Bring the stock to a boil in a saucepan. Blend the tomatoes, stock and tarragon in a blender. Add 1/4 cup olive oil in a fine stream, blending constantly. Season with salt and pepper.

For the salmon, preheat the grill. Combine the lemon juice, ancho chile flakes and honey in a small saucepan. Bring to a boil and remove from the heat. Brush the salmon lightly with oil and season with salt and pepper. Place on a grill rack and grill until the salmon nearly tests done. Brush with the honey glaze. Continue to grill until the glaze caramelizes and the salmon flakes easily. The glaze will darken quickly, so be careful not to overcook.

To serve, ladle the sauce in the center of four large dinner plates and top each with a salmon fillet. Place the potatoes in the position of twelve o'clock and six o'clock on each plate. Place the fennel in the position of three o'clock and nine o'clock on each plate.

Serves 4

Roasted Fingerling Potatoes

1¹/2 pounds fingerling potatoes
1 tablespoon olive oil
1 tablespoon finely chopped garlic
¹/4 teaspoon sea salt or fine salt
¹/8 teaspoon freshly ground pepper

Preheat the oven to 350 degrees. Toss the potatoes with the olive oil, garlic, sea salt and pepper in a bowl and spoon into a baking pan. Roast for 15 to 20 minutes or until tender.

Serves 4

Grilled Fennel

2 fennel bulbs, cut into halves
1 tablespoon olive oil
Salt and pepper to taste

Preheat the grill. Toss the fennel with the olive oil, salt and pepper in a bowl and place on a grill rack. Grill until tender.
Note: You may also place on a rack in a broiler pan and broil until tender.

Serves 4

Brownie Puddle

Brownie Tart
3/4 cup (1 1/2 sticks) unsalted butter
3 ounces semisweet chocolate
1/2 cup baking cocoa
1/2 cup sugar
3 eggs
2 teaspoons vanilla extract
3 ounces cream cheese, softened
1/2 cup all-purpose flour
Pinch of salt
1 unbaked (9-inch) tart shell

Ganache
1/2 cup heavy cream
4 ounces bittersweet chocolate, chopped
1 teaspoon light corn syrup

Assembly
4 ounces pecan pieces, toasted

For the brownie tart, preheat the oven to 350 degrees. Melt the butter and chocolate in a large heatproof bowl over simmering water. Beat in the baking cocoa. Add the sugar, eggs and vanilla and mix well. Mix the cream cheese, flour and salt in a bowl. Add to the chocolate mixture and mix well. Pour into the unbaked tart shell. Bake for 20 minutes.

For the ganache, heat the cream in a small saucepan over medium heat until the cream begins to simmer around the edge. Remove from the heat and add the chocolate and corn syrup. Let stand for 5 to 7 minutes and stir until smooth.

To assemble, poke holes in the tart with the handle of a wooden spoon and pour some of the ganache into the holes. Let stand until cool. Glaze with the remaining ganache and sprinkle with the pecans. Let stand until set before serving.

Serves 8

ARIZONA INN
"The Best of the Best"

The Arizona Inn celebrated its 75th Anniversary in December 2005. It was built by noted philanthropist and Arizona's first Congresswoman, Isabella Greenway, in 1930. Her goal was to continue helping disabled veterans from the First World War by preserving their jobs at the "Arizona Hut," a furniture factory she had started in Tucson in the late 1920s.

The furniture sold well until the stock market crash in 1929. Always the innovator and problem solver, Mrs. Greenway stepped in and built the Arizona Inn to create a customer to buy the furniture; this kept the factory running. Today, preservation of the Inn's signature furniture is ongoing through the work of two master craftsmen and a painter in an on-site cabinet shop. They also create custom furniture, copy original Hut pieces, and preserve the Greenway family antique collection and period pieces displayed for visitors to enjoy in their guest rooms and public space.

The art collection that graces the walls include Mrs. Greenway's original hand-colored George Catlin lithographs, Audubon prints and other notable artists' work.

The large, formal dining room has a cathedral ceiling, antique sideboards and a center table with a large flower arrangement. The tables are set with white linen, blue goblets and silver flatware. The ladder-back chairs, original Hut furniture, are from 1930. French doors open onto an outside patio dining area. Today's cuisine is American international with southwestern touches evolving from the Inn's long tradition of French culinary prepared offerings.

A pianist plays each evening in the Audubon Bar whose feel is much like a scene from the movie *Casablanca*, with Moorish overtones, bamboo McGuire chairs and marble-topped tables. The recent renovation uncovered and restored recessed wall murals and also added certain modern amenities without losing the wonderful historic feel of a 1930s resort.

Members of the Greenway family have owned and managed the Inn through four generations including today's great-grandson, Will Conroy, and granddaughter, Patty Doar. Mrs. Greenway's original aim was to offer guests a "sophisticated desert retreat that provides peace, privacy and sunshine." Located in central Tucson, the Inn is a "14-acre oasis of tranquility and is open year round." Truly, "the best of the best," according to the *Condé Nast* Traveler Gold List.

BREAKFAST MENU

Freshly Squeezed Orange Juice

◆ Southwestern Breakfast

◆ Black Currant Scones

DINNER MENU

◆ Pumpkin and Butternut Squash Soup

◆ Medallions of Beef with Burgundy and Port Sauce

◆ Spinach and Red Onion Sauté

◆ Roasted Portobello Mushrooms

◆ Mashed Potatoes

Ginger Cappuccino Ice Cream

◆ Madeleines

◆ *Recipes Included*

Arizona Inn

Southwestern Breakfast

4 blue corn tortillas, heated
4 (6-inch) flour tortillas, heated
1¹/2 cups refried beans, heated
Tomatillo Sauce (below)
8 eggs
1¹/2 cups (6 ounces) shredded
   Cheddar cheese

4 scallions, chopped
1 cup chopped tomatoes
4 chorizo links
4 lime slices
4 serrano chiles

Place one blue corn tortilla, one flour tortilla and one-fourth of the refried beans next to each other on each of four serving plates. Ladle the tomatillo sauce over the tortillas. Fry the eggs in a skillet to the desired degree of doneness and place one fried egg on top of each tortilla. Sprinkle with the cheese, scallions and tomatoes. Cook the sausage links in a skillet until cooked through. Place a sausage link, lime slice and serrano chile on each plate.

Serves 4

Tomatillo Sauce

12 small tomatillos
1 white onion, chopped
1 tablespoon olive oil
¹/4 cup fresh cilantro, chopped
¹/2 teaspoon ground coriander

¹/2 teaspoon ground cumin
2 garlic cloves, minced
2 tablespoons water
Salt and pepper to taste

Remove the husks from the tomatillos and chop coarsely. Sauté the onion in the olive oil in a large saucepan over medium heat until soft but not brown. Add the tomatillos, cilantro, coriander, cumin, garlic and water. Cook for 7 to 10 minutes or until tender. Process in a blender until smooth. Season with salt and pepper.

Serves 4

Black Currant Scones

2 cups all-purpose flour
1/2 teaspoon salt
1 tablespoon baking powder
2 tablespoons sugar

1/4 cup (1/2 stick) unsalted butter
1/2 cup dried black currants
1/2 cup cream
1 egg, beaten

Preheat the oven to 450 degrees. Sift the flour, salt, baking powder and sugar into a bowl. Cut in the butter until crumbly using a pastry blender. Stir in the currants. Blend the cream with the beaten egg and stir into the flour mixture using a fork. Do not overmix. Divide the dough into three balls. Pat each ball into a circle 1/2 inch thick and cut into the desired shapes. Place on an ungreased baking sheet. Bake for 12 minutes or until golden brown.

Makes 12 to 18

ARIZONA INN DINNER MENU

Pumpkin and Butternut Squash Soup

1/2 onion, chopped
2 tablespoons olive oil
2 butternut squash, peeled
   and chopped
2 cups water, or as needed

1 1/2 cups pumpkin purée
1/2 to 1 teaspoon grated nutmeg
1/4 cup plus 2 tablespoons honey
2 cups heavy cream
Salt and pepper to taste

Sauté the onion in the olive oil in a large stockpot over medium heat for 2 to 3 minutes or until translucent. Add the squash and half the water and cook for 10 to 15 minutes. Stir in the pumpkin purée, nutmeg and honey. Cook for 15 minutes or until the squash is soft and cooked through, adding the remaining water if needed to reach the desired consistency. Blend in batches in a blender until smooth, straining each batch to remove the solids and fibers. Return to the stockpot and stir in the cream. Cook until heated through, stirring occasionally. Season with salt and pepper and add additional honey or nutmeg, if desired. Ladle into soup bowls. Garnish each serving with a swirl of heavy cream and pumpkin seeds.

Serves 4

Medallions of Beef with Burgundy and Port Sauce

Burgundy and Port Sauce
- 1 tablespoon minced shallots
- 1 tablespoon olive oil
- 1 cup port
- 1 cup burgundy
- 2 sprigs of fresh thyme
- 1 bay leaf
- 6 whole black peppercorns
- 1/4 bunch Italian parsley leaves
- 1 quart veal stock
- Salt and pepper to taste

Beef
- 4 (4-ounce) beef medallions
- Salt and pepper to taste
- Vegetable oil
- 1/2 cup burgundy
- Spinach and Red Onion Sauté (below)
- Roasted Portobello Mushrooms (page 108)
- Mashed Potatoes (page 108)

For the sauce, sauté the shallots in the olive oil in a medium saucepan until translucent. Add the wines, thyme, bay leaf, peppercorns and parsley. Cook until the liquid has almost completely evaporated. Add the stock. Cook until the mixture is reduced by half to attain a light sauce consistency. Strain the sauce to remove all solids and season with salt and pepper.

For the beef, preheat the oven to 400 degrees. Season the beef on both sides with salt and pepper. Pour enough oil into an ovenproof sauté pan to coat the bottom and add the beef. Cook over high heat until brown. Turn over the beef and remove from the heat. Pour the wine over the beef and bake to the desired degree of doneness.

To serve, place one-fourth of the spinach and red onion sauté in the center of each plate and top with a roasted portobello mushroom. Place the beef on top of the mushroom and pipe rosettes of mashed potatoes in even amounts onto each plate in the position of twelve o'clock, three o'clock, six o'clock and nine o'clock. Ladle 2 to 3 ounces of the sauce on each plate.

Serves 4

Spinach and Red Onion Sauté

- 1 1/2 cups sliced red onions
- 1 tablespoon olive oil
- 8 cups spinach leaves, chopped
- Salt and pepper to taste

Sauté the onions in the olive oil in a sauté pan over high heat for 1 minute. Add the spinach and sauté just until wilted. Season with salt and pepper.

Serves 4

Roasted Portobello Mushrooms

1/4 cup olive oil
2 teaspoons minced garlic
4 teaspoons minced shallots
1 tablespoon chopped fresh parsley
1 1/2 teaspoons chopped fresh basil
1 1/2 teaspoons chopped fresh chives
Salt and pepper to taste
4 portobello mushrooms, gills scraped
1/4 cup white wine

Preheat the oven to 350 degrees. Mix the olive oil, garlic, shallots, parsley, basil, chives, salt and pepper in a bowl. Add the mushrooms and toss to coat. Place the mushrooms in a shallow baking dish. Pour the wine over the mushrooms and cover with foil. Roast for 15 minutes and remove the foil. Roast for 5 minutes longer. Remove from the oven and keep warm until ready to serve.

Serves 4

Mashed Potatoes

1 quart water
2 tablespoons salt
4 russet potatoes, scrubbed and cut into large pieces
1 cup heavy cream
3 tablespoons unsalted butter
Kosher salt to taste
White pepper to taste

Bring the water to a boil in a large saucepan and add 2 tablespoons salt. Add the potatoes and cook for 10 minutes or until tender and cooked through. Heat the cream and butter in a saucepan until the butter melts. Drain the potatoes and force through a food mill or ricer into a bowl. Stir in enough of the cream mixture to make a creamy yet firm mixture. Season with kosher salt and white pepper. Keep warm until ready to serve.

Serves 4

Madeleines

1/2 cup (1 stick) plus 1 tablespoon butter, softened
1 1/4 cups granulated sugar
1/2 cup all-purpose flour
1/2 cup cake flour
1/2 cup ground almonds
6 eggs
1 teaspoon salt
2 tablespoons orange flower water
2 tablespoons vanilla extract
Confectioners' sugar

Cook the butter in a saucepan until golden brown. Cool to room temperature. Combine the granulated sugar, all-purpose flour, cake flour and almonds in a bowl and stir to mix. Whisk the eggs and salt in a bowl until thick. Whisk in the orange flower water and vanilla. Add the flour mixture and butter alternately, whisking constantly. Chill the dough for 1 hour or until firm.

Preheat the oven to 450 degrees. Spoon the dough into a pastry bag without a tip. Pipe the dough to just under the rim in buttered madeleine molds. Bake for 8 minutes or until the cakes are spongy and golden brown. Cool completely in the molds. Remove from the molds and sprinkle with confectioners' sugar.

Makes about 15

THE COPPER QUEEN HOTEL
"Food Worth Driving Back For"

Work began by the Phelps Dodge Corporation on "The Famous Old Queen" in 1898 by blasting away a solid rock portion of the mountainside. The fashionable hotel with an Italian flair opened its doors in February 1902 in Bisbee, the southernmost mile-high city and, at one point, the largest city between San Francisco and St. Louis. This was during the busy years of the "roaring twenties." Today, the quieter ambience of historic Bisbee functions without a single traffic light.

Over a hundred years ago, the original hotel had 73 rooms with guests sharing a common bathroom at the end of the hall on each floor. The lobby was laid with Italian mosaic tile, and a small portion remains today at the entrance. The safe behind the front desk was once used at the Phelps Dodge Copper mine and held the mine's total cash payroll.

The Copper Queen's walls are nearly two feet thick, keeping the building relatively cool during the summer. An elevator was added during the 1940s, and a swimming pool was built 30 years later. The Victorian Saloon boasts the back bar from Old Kentucky Homestead, a historic bar on Brewery Gulch. Everyone loves the nearly life-size nude portrait of Lily Langtry, a famous stage actress who was one of the mistresses of the Prince of Wales, later King Edward VII.

Winchester's Restaurant, decorated with lace curtains and antiques, can no longer provide a T-bone steak for $1.25, but today's diners enjoy an up-to-date menu in Bisbee's only full service hotel.

DINNER MENU

Maximillian Salad

◆ Potato Dijon Soup

◆ Salmon Roulade

◆ Macaroon Nut Tart

◆ *Recipes Included*

Potato Dijon Soup

1 onion, chopped
2 leeks, cleaned and sliced (white part only)
3 ounces pancetta, chopped
6 cups chicken broth
3 russet potatoes, peeled
2 tablespoons Dijon mustard
1 cup heavy cream or half-and-half
Salt and pepper to taste

Sweat the onion, leeks and pancetta in a stockpot. Add the broth and potatoes and bring to a boil. Cook over medium heat for 15 minutes or until tender. Add the Dijon mustard. Simmer for 5 minutes. Purée 1 cup of the soup at a time in a food processor fitted with a steel blade. Return to the stockpot and add the cream. Cook over low heat until heated through. Season with salt and pepper.

Note: Sweating is cooking a food (typically vegetables) in a small amount of fat, usually covered, over low heat without browning until the food softens and releases moisture; sweating allows the food to release its flavor more quickly when it is later cooked with other foods.

Serves 6

Salmon Roulade

2 ounces oil-pack sun-dried tomatoes, julienned
3 garlic cloves, minced
2 tablespoons olive oil
12 ounces spinach
6 (4- to 5-ounce) wild salmon fillets, skin removed
2 cups riesling
3/4 cup heavy cream

Preheat the oven to 350 degrees. Sauté the sun-dried tomatoes and garlic in the olive oil in a small skillet. Sauté the spinach in a skillet until wilted. Drain the spinach, squeezing out the excess moisture. Add the spinach to the sautéed tomato mixture and mix well. Divide evenly among the fillets on the side the skin was on and roll up. Place seam side down in an 8×8-inch baking dish and cover with the wine. Cover and bake for 10 minutes or until the fish flakes easily.

Drain the salmon, reserving the liquid. Cook the reserved liquid in a saucepan until reduced to 1/4 cup. Stir in the cream. Cook over medium heat for 5 minutes or until thickened, stirring constantly. Spoon 1 tablespoon of the sauce over each roulade. Garnish with finely chopped red bell pepper.

Serves 6

Macaroon Nut Tart

Crust
1¹/₃ cups all-purpose flour
¹/₂ cup (1 stick) unsalted butter,
    chilled and cut into 1-inch pieces
1 teaspoon salt
¹/₄ cup ice water

Tart
6 tablespoons unsalted butter
¹/₂ cup packed brown sugar
4 egg yolks, beaten
1 cup shredded coconut, toasted
¹/₂ cup milk
1 teaspoon vanilla extract
¹/₂ cup macadamia nuts, chopped
¹/₄ cup almonds, chopped

For the crust, process the flour, butter and salt in a food processor fitted with a metal blade for 8 to 10 seconds or until the mixture has the consistency of coarse cornmeal. Add the ice water in a steady stream, processing constantly until the pastry forms a ball. If the pastry is too sticky, add additional flour 1 tablespoon at a time, processing constantly. Wrap the pastry immediately in plastic wrap and chill in the refrigerator. Roll the pastry ¹/₈ inch thick on a floured board. Chill before baking to prevent shrinkage.

Preheat the oven to 425 degrees. Fit the pastry into a 9-inch tart pan. Cover with a circle of waxed paper and fill with 2 cups metal pie weights or uncooked dried beans. Bake for 15 to 20 minutes or until golden brown. Remove the waxed paper and weights and cool before filling.

For the tart, reduce the oven temperature to 350 degrees. Melt the butter in a saucepan and stir in the brown sugar. Add the egg yolks, coconut, milk and vanilla and mix well. Pour into the cooled baked crust and top with the macadamia nuts and almonds. Bake for 20 to 25 minutes or until set. Cool to room temperature and chill until ready to serve. Garnish each serving with a dollop of whipped cream and toasted coconut.

Serves 8

Rancho de La Osa

"Come, and Listen to the Silence."

It was here that Father Eusebio Francisco Kino, and his followers, founded and built a Jesuit mission outpost in the late 1600s. This building was used to trade with the local Indians and Mexicans for more than a century, and this rare and historic adobe structure may be the oldest building in Arizona.

Rancho de La Osa is part of the original 3,000,000-acre land grant from the King of Spain to the Ortiz brothers of Mexico in 1812. Secluded among huge, old eucalyptus trees, Ranch of the "She Bear," was built between 1830 and 1870, and is one of the last great Spanish haciendas standing in the United States. To settle an ongoing border dispute, the Gadsden Purchase was signed in 1854, and the ranch fell within the U.S. boundaries.

Mexican Revolution leader Poncho Villa is reported to have fired on the hacienda. A Mexican cannonball was found embedded in the stucco walls of the main house where it is displayed.

In 1921, Louise Wade Wetherill, a Navajo historian, came south to southern Arizona looking for a lost tribe of Navajos. She never found them, but she started "Hacienda de La Osa Guest Ranch." Over the years, the Ranch became a getaway for luminaries such as President Lyndon Johnson, Adlai Stevenson, William O. Douglas, movie cowboys Tom Mix and John Wayne and Georgia's famous author, Margaret Mitchell.

Boasting sunshine for 300 days each year, the Ranch is bordered by the Buenos Aires National Wildlife Refuge where herds of deer and antelope roam freely.

BREAKFAST MENU

◆ Berry Fruit Salad with Mint Sugar

◆ Southwestern Bacon and Cheese Strata

◆ Very Lemon Bread

Freshly Squeezed Juice

Coffee

DINNER MENU

◆ Bibb Lettuce with Avocado and Toasted Pine Nut Salad

◆ Piñon-Crusted Chicken with Cherry Chipotle Sauce

◆ Individual Sweet Potato Soufflés

◆ Oven-Roasted Asparagus

Rolls

◆ Margarita Pie

◆ *Recipes Included*

Rancho de La Osa

Berry Fruit Salad with Mint Sugar

1/2 cup loosely packed fresh mint
6 tablespoons sugar
3 cups sliced strawberries

3 cups blackberries
3 cups blueberries

Pulse the mint and sugar in a food processor until finely ground. Sprinkle over the strawberries, blackberries and blueberries in a large bowl and toss gently to combine. Let stand for 5 minutes before serving.

Serves 8

Southwestern Bacon and Cheese Strata

10 cups cubed trimmed white bread
14 eggs, beaten
4 cups milk or half-and-half
16 slices honey- or mesquite-flavored thick bacon, cooked and crumbled
1 teaspoon white pepper
1 teaspoon dry mustard, or 1 tablespoon Dijon mustard
1 tablespoon finely chopped seeded jalapeño chile
2 cups (8 ounces) shredded sharp Cheddar cheese
2 cups (8 ounces) shredded Monterey Jack cheese

Mix the bread, eggs and milk in a large bowl and let stand for 20 minutes. Add the crumbled bacon, white pepper, dry mustard, jalapeño chile, Cheddar cheese and Monterey Jack cheese and mix well. Spoon into a 9×13-inch baking dish sprayed with nonstick cooking spray. Cover with plastic wrap and chill for 8 to 10 hours. Remove from the refrigerator 30 minutes before baking and place the dish on a baking sheet for ease in handling and for catching any spills.

Preheat the oven to 375 degrees for 15 minutes. Bake the strata for 45 to 60 minutes or until the center is firm and the top is golden brown. Serve with a dollop of sour cream and a drizzle of salsa.

Serves 8

Very Lemon Bread

Bread
1 1/2 cups sifted all-purpose flour
1 teaspoon salt
1 teaspoon baking powder
1 cup sugar
1/3 cup butter, melted
1 1/2 tablespoons lemon extract
2 eggs
1/2 cup milk
1 tablespoon grated lemon zest
1/2 cup pecans, chopped

Lemon Glaze
1/4 cup lemon juice
1/2 cup confectioners' sugar

For the bread, preheat the oven to 350 degrees. Sift the flour, salt and baking powder into a bowl. Mix the sugar, butter and lemon extract in a large bowl. Beat in the eggs. Add the flour mixture and milk alternately, beating until just blended after each addition. Fold in the lemon zest and pecans. Pour into a greased and floured 5×8-inch loaf pan. Bake for 45 minutes or until a wooden pick inserted in the center comes out clean. Cool in the pan on a wire rack for 10 minutes.

For the glaze, blend the lemon juice and confectioners' sugar in a bowl until smooth. Drizzle over the cracks in the warm bread that form while baking.

Makes 1 loaf

Bibb Lettuce with Avocado and Toasted Pine Nut Salad

Orange Vinaigrette
$1/2$ cup extra-virgin olive oil
2 tablespoons white wine vinegar
2 tablespoons fresh orange juice
1 tablespoon Dijon mustard
Salt and freshly ground pepper to taste

Salad
2 heads Bibb lettuce, separated into leaves
3 avocados, seeded and sliced
$1/3$ cup pine nuts, toasted
Wedge of asiago or Parmesan cheese

For the vinaigrette, whisk the olive oil, vinegar, orange juice and Dijon mustard in a small bowl to blend. Season with salt and pepper.

For the salad, place five lettuce leaves on each of six plates. Arrange the sliced avocados and pine nuts atop the lettuce leaves. Shave the cheese using a vegetable peeler and sprinkle over the salad. Drizzle with the vinaigrette.

Serves 6

Piñon-Crusted Chicken with Cherry Chipotle Sauce

Chicken

1 1/2 cups pine nuts, toasted and coarsely chopped (pinon)
2/3 cup bread crumbs
6 garlic cloves, minced
6 tablespoons finely chopped fresh parsley
3 tablespoons dried basil
1 teaspoon salt
1/2 teaspoon white pepper
8 boneless skinless chicken breasts, lightly pounded
1 cup all-purpose flour
4 eggs, beaten
1/2 cup olive oil

Cherry Chipotle Sauce

3 cups canned or frozen Bing cherries, drained and rinsed
1/4 cup sugar
3/4 cup ruby port
1 canned whole chipotle chile in adobo sauce, rinsed, or to taste

For the chicken, preheat the oven to 200 degrees. Mix the pine nuts, bread crumbs, garlic, parsley, basil, salt and white pepper in a small bowl. Dip the chicken into the flour, the beaten eggs and the bread crumb mixture in the order listed to coat. Sauté the coated chicken in the olive oil in a large skillet over medium-high heat for 4 to 5 minutes per side or until cooked through and golden brown. Remove to an ovenproof platter. Cover with foil and place in the preheated oven to keep warm.

For the sauce, combine the cherries, sugar, wine and whole chipotle chile in a small saucepan and bring to a simmer. Simmer until the sugar is dissolved, stirring occasionally. Process in a blender or food processor until puréed. Strain through a fine sieve into a bowl. Serve warm over the chicken.

Serves 8

Individual Sweet Potato Soufflés

4 pounds sweet potatoes
1/2 cup (1 stick) unsalted butter, cut into pieces and softened
3/4 cup sugar
4 eggs
6 tablespoons self-rising flour
1 (12-ounce) can evaporated skim milk,
    or 1 1/2 cups heavy cream
1/4 teaspoon salt
1 teaspoon vanilla extract
1 teaspoon coconut extract
1 teaspoon orange extract

Preheat the oven to 350 degrees. Bake the sweet potatoes until tender. Maintain the oven temperature. Peel the sweet potatoes. Place in a mixing bowl and beat until smooth. Beat in the butter and sugar. Add the eggs one at a time, beating constantly. Add the flour, evaporated milk, salt and flavorings and beat well. Spray eight 4-ounce individual ramekins with cooking spray. Fill halfway with the sweet potato mixture. Bake for 45 minutes or until a knife inserted in the soufflés comes out clean. Cool in the ramekins for 10 minutes. Invert onto serving plates or serve in the ramekins. Garnish each soufflé with a pecan half.

Serves 8

Oven-Roasted Asparagus

48 thin asparagus spears
Extra-virgin olive oil
White pepper to taste

Preheat the oven to 400 degrees. Trim the asparagus to the desired length, making sure to cut off and discard the tough ends. Group into six spears per guest on a baking sheet lined with baking parchment paper. Drizzle with olive oil and sprinkle with white pepper. Bake for 5 minutes or until tender-crisp. Remove with tongs to serving plates.

Note: You may use thirty-two thick asparagus spears and group into four spears per guest. Bake for 8 to 10 minutes or until tender-crisp.

Serves 8

Margarita Pie

Pretzel Crust
    1 1/2 cups finely crushed pretzels
    1 cup sugar
    1/2 cup (1 stick) butter, melted

Pie
    1/2 cup fresh lime juice
    1 (14-ounce) can sweetened condensed milk
    2 tablespoons gold tequila
    2 tablespoons Triple Sec
    2 cups heavy whipping cream, whipped
    Green food coloring (optional)

For the crust, pulse the pretzels and sugar in a food processor several times to combine. Add the butter in a steady stream and process until well mixed. Press over the bottom and up the side of a 9-inch pie plate sprayed with nonstick cooking spray.

For the pie, combine the lime juice, condensed milk, tequila and Triple Sec in a bowl and mix well. Fold in the whipped cream. Tint with green food coloring if you desire a deeper color. Spoon into the crust. Cover with plastic wrap and freeze for 4 hours or up to 1 week. Garnish with additional whipped cream and lime slices.

Note: Do not use fat-free or low-fat pretzels in the crust or the crust will not hold together when cutting. You may substitute graham crackers for the pretzels.

Serves 6 to 8

WHAT IS A HISTORYMAKER™*?

The Historymakers Gala and Recognition Program honors men and women, living when selected, who have distinguished themselves with noted achievements in such diverse areas as the arts, athletics, communications, community service, education, and entertainment and who have maintained their ties to Arizona.

The Historymaker program raises funds with the Galas to support the Arizona Historical Society Museum at Papago Park, contributes to the museum's artifact, oral history and photographic collections and increases public awareness of the museum.

Each Historymaker participates in oral history, video and portrait sessions and donates personal memorabilia to the museum. Honorees are presented at the Gala, usually a biennial event, which features a premier screening of each Historymaker's unique life story and accomplishments.

At the museum, Historymakers' portraits, biographies and artifacts are exhibited on a rotating basis. A comprehensive collection of photographs and oral histories are housed in the library and archives. The program, which began in 1992, has recognized 44 individuals or groups through 2005.

Historymakers is a registered trademark of Historical League, Inc.

2005
Bruce Babbitt
Cloves Campbell, Sr.
(1931–2004)
John Driggs
Navajo Code Talkers
Alberto Rios

2003
Calvin C. Goode
Jack Pfister
Bill Shover
Esther Don Tang
Virginia Ullman
(1907–2005)

2001
Eddie Basha
Jerry Colangelo
Stevie and Karl Eller
Paul J. Fannin
(1908–2002)
John F. Long

1999
Adam Diaz
Robert T. McCall
G. Robert Herberger
(1904–1999) and
Katherine "Kax"
Herberger
(1912–2003)
Rose Mofford
Newton Rosenzweig
(1905–2002)

1997
Roy P. Drachman
(1906–2000)
Bennie Montague
Gonzales
Del Lewis and
Jewel Lewis
(1929–2003)
Polly Rosenbaum
(1899–2003)
Morrison F. Warren
(1923–2002)

1995
Ben Avery
(1909–1996)
Joe Beeler
(1931–2006)
Tom Chauncey
(1913–1996)
J. Lawrence Walkup
(1914–2002)
Mark Wilmer
(1903–1994)

1993
Erma Bombeck
(1927–1996)
Edward "Bud" Jacobson
(1922–2005)
William "Bill" Masao
Kajikawa
Dwight "Pat" Patterson
(1912–1999)
John Jacob Rhodes, Jr.
(1916–2003)
John "Jack" R. Williams
(1909–1998)

1992
Phillip C. Curtis
(1907–2000)
Barry M. Goldwater
(1909–1998)
Robert W. Goldwater, Sr.
J. Eugene Grigsby, Jr.
Sandra Day O'Connor
Bil Keane
Frank Snell
(1899–1994)
The Wallace and
Ladmo Team:
Bill Thompson
Ladmo Kwiatkowski
(1928–1994)
Pat McMahon

Historymakers

This recipe was submitted by Gail Driggs, John's wife. She recalls that during the 1950s everyone went to Mrs. Van Zant's Poncho's Patio, a restaurant on North Central, above Camelback Road, to enjoy her delicious Mexican food. The Driggs family often gives these wonderful green corn tamales as gifts at Christmas.

JOHN DRIGGS
Historymaker 2005

John Driggs' career was in the family banking business, but he has devoted much of his life to community service. He served as mayor of Phoenix for two terms and entered the campaign as a Republican candidate for governor. A native Arizonan, Driggs' passion is historic preservation. He led efforts to restore the Rossen House and create Heritage Square in downtown Phoenix. Currently, Driggs is spearheading efforts to renovate Papago Park and Tovrea Castle, and he is actively involved in planning celebrations for Arizona's 2012 statehood centennial.

Green Corn Tamales

2 1/2 cups masa or masa harina, prepared
1 1/2 teaspoons baking powder
1 1/2 teaspoons salt
1/2 cup lard
Beef broth
2 dozen cornhusks
1 (12-ounce) can dry vacuum-pack whole kernel corn

2 cups (8 ounces) shredded Cheddar cheese
1/4 cup (or more) diced green chiles
2 tablespoons sugar, or to taste
2 tablespoons butter
Salt to taste

Mix the masa, baking powder and 1 1/2 teaspoons salt in a bowl. Cut in the lard until crumbly. Add enough broth to make the dough stiff enough to handle. Rinse and clean the cornhusks. Soak the husks in enough water to cover in a large container. Drain and pat dry. Drain the corn, reserving the liquid. Process 1 cup of the masa mixture, the corn and remaining ingredients in a food processor until combined. Add the reserved corn liquid or milk as needed if the mixture appears too dry. Spoon 2 tablespoons of the corn filling on the smooth side of each husk and roll up to enclose the filling. Turn up the small ends of the husks and stand in a steamer. Cover with waxed paper and a dampened kitchen towel and steam for 30 to 45 minutes or until the corn is clear and the filling is firm.

Makes 2 dozen tamales

ESTHER DON TANG
Historymaker 2003

Esther Don Tang is a dynamic community leader and successful businesswoman in Tucson. A native Arizonan, she lives by her Chinese immigrant parents' philosophy that the community is your home and you work to improve it. Tang and her husband David built a prosperous chain of grocery stores and drugstores in Tucson. She volunteers for a wide variety of community causes and organizations, including the YWCA, Democratic Party and Catholic Church. As a community activist, she promotes diversity and tolerance of age, ethnic and religious differences.

Nuevo Menudo (Chinese Style)

4 beef hooves
8 ounces garlic cloves
5 gallons water
10 pounds tripe, cut into small pieces
2 pounds mari-guts, cut into 1-inch pieces (optional)
5 pounds raw hominy, rinsed and cooked
Salt to taste
Chopped fresh cilantro
Chopped green onions
Chiltepín (optional)

Combine the hooves, garlic and water in a 10-gallon stockpot and bring to a boil. Boil for 3 hours. Add the tripe and mari-guts and return to a boil. Boil for 1½ hours or until tender. Stir in the hominy and salt. Cook for 30 minutes longer. Serve hot with cilantro, green onions and chiltepín.

Serves 10 to 15

"It has been a tradition in our family since we were children to have an enormous pot of menudo with Chinese goodies to start the New Year," says Esther. She is 88 years old, active and believes that Father Kino must have had a Chinese cook because everything originated from China except coffee.

Printed in Historical Padre Kino Cookbook, October 1991.

"As long as I can remember, tabouli salad was a favorite in our family regardless of the day of the week or season of the year. This culinary and Lebanese delight continues to be a most popular salad of the Basha family."

EDDIE BASHA
Historymaker 2001

Eddie Basha is head of Arizona's only family-owned supermarket chain and grandson of Lebanese immigrants. He has given generously to his home state in the name of education and children. A multifaceted man, Basha also avidly collects contemporary Western American and Native American art. He has served as a leader of many civic groups as well as educational and charitable organizations. He also ventured into the world of Arizona politics where he made a near-miss run as the Democratic candidate for governor.

Tabouli Salad

1/2 cup cracked wheat
4 tomatoes, chopped
3 bunches parsley, stemmed and chopped
1 bunch green onions, sliced
Small handful of fresh mint, stemmed and chopped
1/2 cup olive oil
1/2 cup lemon juice
Salt and freshly ground pepper to taste

Soak the cracked wheat in enough water to generously cover in a bowl for 30 minutes and drain. Press the excess moisture from the cracked wheat. Combine the cracked wheat, tomatoes, parsley, green onions and mint in a bowl and mix well. Stir in the olive oil and lemon juice and season to taste with salt and pepper. Delicious served cupped in any variety of lettuce or fresh grape leaves.

Serves 6 to 8

PAUL J. FANNIN
1908–2002
Historymaker 2001

Paul Fannin served the state of Arizona as both Governor and United States Senator. A successful businessman, he was urged to run for governor as a Republican when Democrats outnumbered Republicans six to one. He was elected and served three terms. As Senator, it was his energy and extensive knowledge of Arizona, working with Senator Carl Hayden, which helped secure Arizona's future needs for more water with the Central Arizona Project. His personal motto said it all: "Let the other fellow have the credit, if that's going to get the job done."

Beef Stew

1 pound sirloin steak, cubed, or beef stew meat
4 (14-ounce) cans beef broth
1 green bell pepper, cut into quarters
2 ribs celery
1 onion, cut into halves
2 garlic cloves
Dash of pepper
2 potatoes, peeled and coarsely chopped
2 carrots, peeled and sliced
1 cup frozen peas or green beans

Bring the steak, broth, bell pepper, celery, onion, garlic and pepper to a boil in a stockpot and reduce the heat. Simmer for 3 to 4 hours or until the steak is tender, stirring occasionally. Discard the bell pepper quarters, celery and garlic cloves. Add the potatoes, carrots, peas and/or any other vegetable to the stew and cook until the potatoes are tender, adding additional broth as needed for the desired consistency and stirring occasionally. Ladle into bowls.

Serves 4 to 5

This recipe favorite was contributed by "Cookie" Ploegsma, the Fannins' long-time cook who believed the Senator was a man of simple taste and pleasures, kind, caring and jovial. Both Mr. and Mrs. Fannin enjoyed Cookie's special hot dogs, and he frequently requested her beef stew and chili. Cookie treasures her memories and is ever grateful for their friendship.

Kax and Bob moved to Arizona in 1949 with their children, Judd, Gail and Gary. Bob bought lots of desert land and the family explored it often by jeep and on horseback. They entertained their neighbors and visitors from the Midwest, taking them on picnics with a backdrop of natural beauty and pristine desert. Judd remembers a simple, yet refreshing salad his mother liked to bring.

From Judd Herberger

G. ROBERT "BOB" HERBERGER
1904–1999
Historymaker 1999

KATHERINE K. "KAX" HERBERGER
1912–2003
Historymaker 1999

Robert and Kax Herberger were lifelong philanthropists, contributing to a wide range of community achievements. A successful businessman, Robert founded department stores and a wholesale company in the Midwest. Moving to Phoenix in 1949, the Herbergers became involved in the Valley community. Robert dedicated his efforts in diverse areas, including organizing the Fiesta Bowl and founding Valley Presbyterian Church, while Katherine had a particular devotion to the arts in Scottsdale, Phoenix and at Arizona State University. Among other contributions, the Herbergers donated land for 31 Valley parks.

Desert Picnic Salad

4 pounds seedless green grapes, cut into halves
4 cups sour cream
1 (1-pound) package brown sugar
2 cups pecan halves

Layer the grapes, sour cream, brown sugar and pecans in a 9×13-inch dish. Chill, covered, for 8 to 10 hours.

Serves 10 to 12

ROSE MOFFORD
Historymaker 1999

Rose Perica Mofford has functioned in a leadership capacity starting as president of her seventh grade class and culminating as first woman Governor of Arizona. A native of Globe, and a Democrat, she spent her entire career in state government including serving as Secretary of State prior to her term as Governor. As a member of the Cantaloupe Queens, an all-American softball team, Mofford was twice inducted into the Arizona Softball Hall of Fame. She has participated in 35 organizations and served on charitable foundation boards.

Cornish Pasties

Pastry
4 cups all-purpose flour
3/4 teaspoon salt
1/2 cup shortening
1 cup beef suet, finely
   chopped
4 to 6 tablespoons ice
   water

Filling and Assembly
2 pounds round steak or
   other lean beef, cut
   into 1/2-inch cubes
2 or 3 potatoes, peeled
   and coarsely chopped
2 or 3 small onions,
   coarsely chopped
Salt and pepper to taste
Butter

For the pastry, mix the flour and salt in a bowl. Cut in the shortening until the mixture resembles cornmeal. Add the suet and toss with a fork until combined. Add just enough of the ice water to make the dough adhere and mix well. Knead lightly and shape the pastry into a ball. Chill, covered, for 1 hour.

For the filling, preheat the oven to 350 degrees. Mix the steak, potatoes, onions, salt and pepper in a bowl. Pat the pastry on a lightly floured surface into 1/4-inch-thick rounds 8 or 9 inches in diameter. Press on the pastry to flatten pieces of the suet. Spoon 1/4 to 1/2 cup of the filling onto half of each dough round and dot with butter. Moisten the edge with water and fold over to enclose the filling. Press the edge with your fingers or a fork to seal. Arrange the pasties on a baking sheet and bake for 1 hour.

Makes 8 pasties

"My wonderful parents, John and Frances Perica, moved to Globe in 1915 where my father was employed at the Old Dominion Mine. Our home was in an English neighborhood and my mother soon learned to make pasties. These were a special treat and served as a full meal. In conversations with friends from the rural areas, they also fondly remember the good old days and delicious pasties. If I have any regrets, it is that I did not learn to make them, as well as save all my mother's recipes to be included in cookbooks."

This favorite recipe came from Roy's mother, Millie Royers Drachman, a French lady who learned to cook everything Mexican after she married Roy's father, Manny. Daughter-in-law Lorraine learned to make the family's favorite from Millie, and keeps the family tradition of serving flat enchiladas every Christmas Eve. Roy's granddaughters (Lorraine's daughters) also serve this family recipe to their own children.

From Lorraine Drachman

ROY P. DRACHMAN
1906–2000
Historymaker 1997

Roy Drachman was synonymous with the development of his native Tucson, contributing to a vast array of civic needs. A major innovator in commercial real estate, he co-developed, with Del Webb, the "shopping center" concept in Tucson and Phoenix. Through his combined love of Tucson and sports, Drachman was instrumental in bringing Spring Baseball to Tucson. A staunch supporter of the University of Arizona, Drachman served on the Alumni Association Board of Directors and founded the Roy P. Drachman Institute for Land and Redevelopment Studies which assists smaller cities with their planning needs.

Flat Enchiladas

2 pounds fresh corn masa
1/2 cup (2 ounces) shredded Cheddar cheese
1 egg
1 teaspoon salt
Vegetable oil for frying
Red Chile Sauce (page 135)
Shredded Cheddar cheese
Chopped green onions
Sliced green olives

Preheat the oven to 350 degrees. Combine the masa, 1/2 cup cheese, the egg and salt in a bowl and mix by hand until combined. Shape the dough into rounds the size of an egg. Arrange the rounds between two sheets of waxed paper and flatten 1/4 inch thick using a rolling pin or tortilla press.

Heat 2 inches of oil in a small skillet and fry each patty for 3 to 5 minutes per side, turning once. Drain on paper towels. Dip each patty in some of the red chile sauce and layer in a 9×13-inch baking dish, generously sprinkling with cheese, green onions and olives between each layer. Bake until heated through; do not overbake. Adjust the recipe for a large crowd. You may substitute dried corn masa using the package directions for the fresh corn masa.

Serves 12 to 15

Red Chile Sauce

1 tablespoon vegetable oil
1 tablespoon all-purpose flour
3 to 4 cups chicken broth or beef broth, heated
1 (16-ounce) jar red chile paste
1 or 2 garlic cloves, chopped
1 teaspoon dried oregano

Heat the oil in a saucepan and whisk in the flour. Cook until the flour is brown, stirring constantly. Add the broth, chile paste, garlic and oregano, stirring constantly. Simmer for 10 to 15 minutes or to the desired consistency, stirring occasionally. Add less broth for a thicker sauce.

Makes 3 cups

Polly and another longtime legislator, Betty Rockwell, were close friends and also shared the same birthday. They often celebrated their birthdays together with their favorite chocolate cake. Polly's family believed she lived on chocolate—she loved See's dark chocolates with soft centers, but no marzipan. This chocolate cake was served on Polly's 100th birthday to both Polly and Betty.

From Judy Stickney, Polly's niece

Polly Rosenbaum, known as the protector of Arizona's heritage, was on the forefront of many projects to preserve its history. Although she arrived in Arizona to teach school in the mining camp of Hayden, during the Depression she worked at the state legislature. She married Bill "Rosey" Rosenbaum, a state representative, and upon his death was appointed to his seat in the Arizona House of Representatives. She continued, as a Democrat, to represent Gila County for the next 45 years. A staunch supporter of educational programs, she worked to approve the community college system for Arizona.

Polly's 100th Birthday Chocolate Cake

2 cups all-purpose flour
2 cups sugar
1 cup water
1/2 cup (1 stick) butter
1/2 cup shortening
1/4 cup (heaping) baking cocoa
1/2 cup buttermilk
1 teaspoon baking soda
2 eggs, lightly beaten
1 teaspoon vanilla extract
Chocolate Icing (page 137)

Preheat the oven to 375 degrees. Mix the flour and sugar in a heatproof bowl. Combine the water, butter, shortening and baking cocoa in a saucepan and bring to a boil, stirring frequently. Pour the hot chocolate mixture over the flour mixture gradually, stirring constantly until smooth.

Mix the buttermilk and baking soda in a measuring cup until blended. Add the buttermilk mixture, eggs and vanilla to the chocolate mixture and mix well.

Pour the batter into a greased and floured 9×13-inch cake pan. Bake for 20 to 25 minutes or until a wooden pick inserted in the center comes out clean. Spread the hot icing over the top of the hot cake. Let stand until set.

Serves 12 to 16

Chocolate Icing

1/2 cup (1 stick) butter
6 tablespoons milk
1/4 cup baking cocoa
1 (1-pound) package confectioners' sugar
1 teaspoon vanilla extract
1 cup chopped pecans

Combine the butter, milk and baking cocoa in a saucepan 5 minutes before the cake tests done and bring to a boil, stirring constantly. Pour over the confectioners' sugar in a heatproof bowl and whisk until smooth. Stir in the vanilla and pecans.

Serves 12 to 16

MARK WILMER
1903–1994
Historymaker 1995

This recipe is Genevieve Wilmer's, Mark's wife, and is from his children: Mark, Charles, Liz Wilmer Sexson and Gen Wilmer Hendricks. Liz remembers that her dad was an early riser and with four children, he must have enjoyed the quiet time. He loved his wife's chicken tamales; she learned to make them from her mother when she was a girl in Ray, Arizona. Her dad owned the general store frequented by the miners. She never followed a recipe so the Wilmer kids had to watch her to write it down. "Dad loved to have two fried eggs with her homemade chicken tamales to start his day. We kids loved them, too."

Mark Wilmer, known as the "Dean of Arizona's Trial Lawyers," was a founding partner in Arizona's largest law firm, Snell and Wilmer. He was the first lawyer in Arizona to be elected to the American College of Trial Lawyers. Wilmer distinguished himself as a litigator at the trial and appellate levels. His most significant professional achievement was successful representation of the State of Arizona before the United States Supreme Court in establishing Arizona's right to a substantial portion of the Colorado River water.

Homemade Chicken Tamales

1 pound cornhusks
1 (4-pound) chicken
1 string of red chiles, stemmed and seeded
4 to 6 quarts water
1 (10-ounce) can enchilada sauce
2 teaspoons salt
1 teaspoon each oregano, ground cumin and
   garlic powder
All-purpose flour
1 1/2 tablespoons shortening
2 (29-ounce) cans hominy (about 6 cups), drained
1/2 cup (1 stick) butter, softened
2 teaspoons salt
2 teaspoons baking powder
3 to 4 dozen pitted black olives

Soak the husks in warm water in a large container. Clean well and drain. Cover the husks with a wet kitchen towel to keep moist. Combine the chicken with enough water to cover in a large stockpot and bring to a boil. Reduce the heat to low and simmer until the chicken comes off the bones. Remove the chicken to a platter, reserving the broth. Cool the chicken slightly and chop into bite-size pieces, discarding the skin and bones. Strain the reserved broth, discarding the solids and skimming off the fat.

Combine the red chiles with 4 to 6 quarts water in a large saucepan and bring to a boil. Remove from the heat and let stand for 45 minutes. Drain, reserving the liquid. Process the red chiles in a food processor until puréed. Strain the purée through a sieve into a saucepan, discarding the solids. Stir in the enchilada sauce, 2 teaspoons salt, the oregano, cumin and garlic powder. Bring to a boil, stirring occasionally. Make a paste in a bowl using equal amounts of flour and water. Mix in the shortening and add to the chile mixture. Cook until the sauce is of a medium consistency, stirring occasionally. Stir in the chicken.

Process the hominy in a food processor until ground. Combine the hominy, reserved strained broth, butter, 2 teaspoons salt and the baking powder in a bowl and mix by hand until combined. Add the reserved chile liquid and additional broth or water if needed for a medium consistency. Spread some of the hominy mixture on each cornhusk along with one black olive. Spoon one heaping spoonful of the chicken mixture in the center of each and fold the bottoms and then the sides of the husks to enclose the filling. Place crushed foil in the bottom of a large saucepan and place a baking rack on top. Fill the saucepan with 2 to 3 inches of water. Stand the tamales up with the bottom folds on the bottom. Bring to a boil and reduce the heat to low. Simmer for 1 to 2 hours or until the hominy mixture (masa) comes away from the husks, adding additional water as needed.

Makes 3 to 4 dozen tamales

In the 1940s, the Wilmer family summered in Pinetop-Lakeside. They liked to eat at Charlie Clark's, then the area's only "nice" place. Because Charlie cooked the steaks and liked to visit with all the diners, the wait was long but the steaks were delicious.

From Liz Wilmer Sexson

This recipe is from Helen Laird Alkire, whose daughter, Alma, served on John's Congressional staff, first as his personal secretary and later as administrative assistant for 25 years, and is still a beloved family friend. It first appeared in the eighth edition of The Congressional Club Cookbook *in 1970 over John's name.*

From Betty Rhodes, John's widow

JOHN J. RHODES, JR.
1916–2003
Historymaker 1993

John Rhodes, a Kansas native, settled in Mesa after World War II and began the law firm of Rhodes and Killian. In November 1952, he was elected to Congress as the first Republican ever elected to the House from the state of Arizona. Rhodes served from 1973–1980 as minority leader of the House where he also was a strong proponent of the Central Arizona Project to bring much needed water to the state. A Congressman for 30 years, he served with eight presidents.

Arizona Date Cake

1 cup dates, chopped	2/3 cup shortening
1 cup boiling water	1 teaspoon vanilla
1 3/4 cups cake flour	extract
2 tablespoons	2 eggs
baking cocoa	1 cup (6 ounces)
1 teaspoon baking soda	semisweet
1/2 teaspoon salt	chocolate chips
1 cup sugar	1 cup pecans, chopped

Preheat the oven to 350 degrees. Mix the dates and boiling water in a heatproof bowl. Let stand until cool. Sift the cake flour, baking cocoa, baking soda and salt together. Beat the sugar and shortening in a bowl of a stand mixer until light and fluffy, scraping the bowl occasionally. Blend in the vanilla. Add the eggs one at a time, beating well after each addition. Add the flour mixture alternately with the undrained dates, beating well after each addition.

Spoon the batter into a greased 9×13-inch cake pan and sprinkle with the chocolate chips and pecans. Bake for 45 minutes. Cool in the pan on a wire rack.

Serves 15

ERMA BOMBECK
1927–1996
Historymaker 1993

Erma Bombeck, noted author and humorist, began her writing career in high school. A lecture tour to Phoenix in 1969 encouraged the Bombeck family to relocate here. Her thrice weekly column, "At Wit's End," was read in newspapers across the United States. For 11 years, Bombeck appeared regularly on Good Morning America *and she wrote numerous best-selling books. Bombeck was also involved in a myriad of local and national charitable causes, including the American Cancer Society and the Arizona Kidney Foundation.*

Tortilla Soup

1 tomato
1/4 cup chopped onion
2 tablespoons chopped fresh cilantro
1/2 teaspoon minced fresh garlic
1 quart chicken broth
8 corn tortillas
Vegetable oil for frying
1/2 avocado, chopped
4 ounces Chihuahua cheese, shredded

Process the tomato, onion, cilantro and garlic in a blender until almost smooth. Pour the tomato mixture into a saucepan and stir in the broth. Bring to a boil over medium-high heat and reduce the heat to low. Simmer, covered, for 20 minutes, stirring occasionally.

Cut the tortillas into 1/2-inch strips and fry in oil in a skillet for 40 to 50 seconds or until crisp and light brown. Drain on paper towels. Divide the tortilla strips, avocado and cheese evenly among four to six soup bowls and ladle the soup into the prepared bowls. Garnish each serving with a sprig of cilantro and serve immediately.

Serves 4 to 6

"I first tasted this soup while on vacation in Cabo San Lucas, Mexico. Since I had eaten it three days straight, the chef was kind enough to give me the recipe. He didn't tell me it fed the Mexican army. Use good sense and start with one tomato, one can of broth and go from there. I never could find Chihuahua cheese, so I use mozzarella, which is disgusting but it tastes good."

From Bill Bombeck, who found this direct quote in Erma's files

This delicious stew was the creation of Josephine "Jo Jo" Goldwater, Barry and Bob's mother. Jo Jo never wrote down this recipe and Barry learned it by peeking over her shoulder and writing what she put in it, guessing at amounts. Peggy, Barry's wife, and he experimented and noted the amounts to create this written recipe. According to Barry, this superb and tasty dish was always served on festive occasions when he was a boy. Crosse and Blackwell pickled walnuts can be found in most gourmet shops.

Submitted by Peggy Goldwater, daughter

BARRY M. GOLDWATER
1909–1998
Historymaker 1992

Barry Goldwater, an Arizona native, was a businessman and Phoenix City Councilman before embarking upon an illustrious career in the United States Senate. In 1964, Goldwater was the Republican candidate for United States President. He was a strong advocate for Native American people and is noted for his photographs of Navajo Indians and the Arizona landscape. Known for his love of ham radio activities and aviation, he served on the U.S. Armed Forces Committee and was instrumental in establishing the Arizona Air National Guard.

Jo Jo's Black Walnut Stew

6 pounds chuck rib roast
1 (14-ounce) can beef broth
1 large onion, cut into halves
1 pound ground round, ground twice
3 jars pickled black walnuts
All-purpose flour
Salt and freshly ground pepper to taste

Combine the roast with the broth and enough water to cover in a Dutch oven. Add the onion and cook over low heat for 4 hours or until the roast is tender. Skim off the fat. Chop or shred the roast.

One hour before serving, shape the ground round into small meatballs. Mash one jar of undrained walnuts in a bowl. Add the meatballs and mashed walnuts to the Dutch oven and mix gently. Whisk in just enough flour to thicken and stir in the remaining two jars of walnuts. Season with salt and pepper. Cook just until heated through. Serve with hot cooked rice or noodles.

Serves 8

ROBERT W. GOLDWATER, SR.
Historymaker 1992

Robert Goldwater, a native of Phoenix, showed great farsightedness in the management and development of the Goldwater department stores. He also worked as a director of Valley National Bank. During World War II, Goldwater served with the Civil Air Patrol. After the war, he and others developed Arizona Airlines, later acquired by Frontier Airlines. Always civic minded, Goldwater is known as the father of the Phoenix Open Golf Tournament, and served on the boards of many business and civic associations.

Maggie Goldwater, Robert Goldwater's wife, submitted this recipe.

Chile Rellenos Casserole

4 (7-ounce) cans whole green chiles
1 pound Monterey Jack cheese
1¹/4 cups milk
5 eggs
¹/4 cup all-purpose flour
Salt and freshly ground pepper to taste
4 cups (16 ounces) shredded mild Cheddar cheese

Preheat the oven to 350 degrees. Slit the green chiles lengthwise on one side. Remove the seeds and drain. Slice the Monterey Jack cheese into 1/4-inch-thick slices and place one slice of the cheese in each slit. Arrange the stuffed green chiles in a greased 9×13-inch baking dish. Whisk the milk, eggs, flour, salt and pepper in a bowl until blended and pour over the stuffed green chiles. Sprinkle with the Cheddar cheese.

Bake for 45 to 60 minutes or until light brown and bubbly, checking after 30 minutes. Cut into squares and serve warm. You may garnish with sour cream, salsa, sliced avocado and/or sliced green onions.

Serves 12

LADIMIR "LADMO" KWIATKOWSKI
1928–1994
Historymaker 1992

Ladmo's mother, "Busha," which means grandmother in Polish, made chruscikis (Polish bow cookies) at Christmas. She taught me, her daughter-in-law, and most of her granddaughters and granddaughters-in-law how to make them. We always had a good time and it usually took all day. Ladmo loved to share these with his friends at KPHO-TV at Christmas.

From Patsy Kwiatkowski, Ladmo's widow

Ladmo Kwiatkowski arrived in Arizona to play baseball at Arizona State University and graduated with a degree in journalism. He joined KPHO-TV and became a cameraman. When Bill Thompson needed a sidekick for his children's television show in 1954, Kwiatkowski was recruited and a phenomenally successful comedy team was born. The Wallace and Ladmo Show, a 36-year record holder as the longest running children's television show in media history, became enormously popular with Arizona children and parents alike. Ladmo made thousands of personal appearances where he distributed "Ladmo Bags" to appreciative audiences and raised millions of dollars for charity.

Chruscikis (Polish Bow Cookies)

3 cups (or more)
   all-purpose flour
1/2 teaspoon baking
   powder
1/2 teaspoon salt
3 tablespoons granulated
   sugar

9 egg yolks
3 tablespoons sour cream
1 teaspoon vanilla extract
Vegetable oil for frying
Confectioners' sugar

Sift 3 cups flour, the baking powder and salt together. Beat the granulated sugar and egg yolks in a mixing bowl until blended. Add the sour cream and vanilla and mix until smooth. Beat in the flour mixture gradually. Knead the dough on a heavily floured surface for 30 minutes, adding in as much additional flour as needed to make the dough no longer sticky. Separate into several portions. Roll each portion very thin, turning frequently. Cut into 1 1/2×4-inch-long strips. Make a slit near one end of each strip and bring the opposite end of the strip through the slit. Heat oil to 375 degrees in a deep-fryer and fry the cookies in the hot oil for a few seconds or until golden, not brown, turning only once. Drain on paper towels and dust with confectioners' sugar.

Makes 8 dozen cookies

Bil Keane, a self-taught artist and cartoonist, began his career as art editor of his high school's magazine. The advent of television led to his drawing of "Channel Chuckles." After he moved to Arizona in 1959, he commenced drawing his award-winning "Family Circus," utilizing his family for subject matter. Keane says, "If there is a philosophy behind the feature, it is that a home filled with love and laughter is the happiest place in the world." He has also used his artistic talent to raise money for numerous charities.

"Good luck with Tastes & Treasures. Love from all of us in the 'Family Circus'."

Lunch at the Museum

Members of the Historical League usually meet monthly on the first Monday.
The meeting begins with lunch, brought by members who volunteer to bring a salad,
an occasional warm casserole, bread or dessert. The luncheons are organized and managed
by the Hospitality Committee; they also set up the salad and dessert buffets.

The luncheon meetings typically have a holiday theme with coordinating paper goods
and fresh flowers, and offer a colorful and appetizing presentation. There is lots of
conversation when members line up to help themselves. This opportunity provides time
for members to discuss League projects, meet new members and renew old friendships.

The variety of salads is endless, prepared by the League's many good cooks who are
always eager to bring something different and interesting. Delectable salads may include
grilled potato, fresh spinach with strawberries, pasta or chicken-curry. The assortment of
artisan breads members enjoy includes ripe olive, crusty French, classic fruit or corn
muffins. And finally, members help themselves to the delicious desserts—
perhaps a slice of lemon loaf, chocolate pie, brownies, summer trifle or an
assortment of home-baked cookies.

Following the bonhomous interaction and good food, the business meetings are held and
members enjoy interesting programs by guest speakers relating to some facet of Arizona
history. Guest speakers are invited to join League members for lunch. Annually,
the Historical League hosts a special lunch for the entire museum staff and awards
grants to the various departments for the coming year.

MENUS

Summer Lunch

Fall Lunch

Winter Lunch

Spring Lunch

Mexican Fiesta

Christmas Lunch

Appreciation Brunch

Lunch at the Museum

Summer Lunch Menu

◆ Gazpacho

◆ Tarragon Chicken Sandwiches

◆ Cashew Pea Salad

◆ Sonoran Potato Salad

◆ Curried Chicken Green Salad

◆ Strawberry Spinach Salad

◆ Chocolate Lover's Delight Pie

◆ Chocolate Sherry Cream Bars

◆ Summer Trifle

◆ Sangria

Gazpacho

5 tomatoes, chopped
1 1/2 cucumbers, chopped
1 green bell pepper, chopped
4 to 6 green onions, sliced
2 garlic cloves, minced
3 cups vegetable juice cocktail

7 tablespoons wine vinegar or white
   balsamic vinegar
6 tablespoons olive oil
1 tablespoon chopped fresh parsley
   or cilantro
Salt and pepper to taste

Combine the tomatoes, cucumbers, bell pepper, green onions and garlic in a bowl and mix well. Stir in the vegetable juice cocktail, vinegar, olive oil and parsley. Season with salt and pepper. Chill, covered, in the refrigerator for 8 to 10 hours. Ladle into bowls or mugs.

Serves 6 to 8

Tarragon Chicken Sandwiches

3 whole chicken breasts
1 teaspoon kosher salt
1/2 teaspoon freshly ground pepper
2 tablespoons vegetable oil
2/3 cup mayonnaise
1/3 cup sliced green onions
1/4 cup smoked almonds, chopped

2 tablespoons chopped fresh tarragon
1/2 teaspoon freshly ground pepper
1/4 teaspoon Dijon mustard
1 loaf whole wheat bread
1 head Bibb lettuce, trimmed and
   separated into leaves

Preheat the oven to 350 degrees. Season the chicken with the kosher salt and 1/2 teaspoon pepper and arrange in a single layer in a 9×13-inch baking dish. Drizzle with the oil, turning to completely coat. Bake for 60 to 80 minutes or until the chicken is cooked through, turning occasionally and checking after 60 minutes. Cool slightly and chop the chicken into bite-size pieces, discarding the skin and bones. This will yield approximately 3 cups.

Combine the mayonnaise, green onions, almonds, tarragon, 1/2 teaspoon pepper and the Dijon mustard in a bowl and mix well. Stir in the chicken and chill, covered, until serving time. To serve, spread the chicken salad on the bread slices and dress with the lettuce.

Serves 6 to 8

Cashew Pea Salad

2 (12-ounce) packages frozen peas,
    thawed and drained
1 (8-ounce) can sliced water
    chestnuts, drained
8 ounces bacon, crisp-cooked and
    crumbled

6 ounces (or more) cashews
2 green onions, finely chopped
1 teaspoon seasoned salt
1 cup sour cream
2 tablespoons mayonnaise

Combine the peas, water chestnuts, bacon, cashews, green onions and seasoned salt in a bowl and mix gently. Stir in a mixture of the sour cream and mayonnaise. Serve immediately or store, covered, in the refrigerator.

Serves 4 to 6

Sonoran Potato Salad

$1^1/2$ to 2 pounds red new potatoes
$1/2$ cup vegetable oil
$1/4$ cup white wine vinegar
1 tablespoon sugar
$1^1/2$ teaspoons chili powder
1 teaspoon seasoned salt
$1/2$ teaspoon garlic salt

$1/4$ teaspoon ground cumin
$1/4$ teaspoon hot red pepper sauce
1 (12-ounce) can Mexicorn, drained
$2/3$ cup thinly sliced green onions
$1/4$ cup sliced black olives
Romaine leaves

Combine the potatoes with enough water to generously cover in a saucepan and bring to a boil. Boil until tender when pierced with a fork; drain. Cool slightly and peel, if desired. Cut the potatoes into $3/4$-inch pieces and place in a bowl.

Whisk the oil, vinegar, sugar, chili powder, seasoned salt, garlic salt, cumin and hot sauce in a bowl until blended. Pour the oil mixture over the warm potatoes and mix until coated. Chill, covered, in the refrigerator. Stir in the corn, green onions and olives and chill, covered, for up to 2 days. Stir just before serving and garnish with romaine leaves.

Serves 4 to 6

Curried Chicken Green Salad

1/2 cup olive oil
1/4 cup red wine vinegar
1/4 cup chutney
1 1/2 teaspoons curry powder
1 teaspoon dry mustard
1/2 teaspoon sugar
1/2 teaspoon salt
2 whole chicken breasts, cooked
    and chopped

10 ounces fresh spring mix
2 Gala apples, chopped
3/4 cup golden raisins
12 fresh mushrooms, sliced
2 or 3 green onions with tops, sliced
1/2 cup pecan halves, toasted
    and chopped

Process the olive oil, vinegar, chutney, curry powder, dry mustard, sugar and salt in a blender until puréed. Chill, covered, in the refrigerator. Toss the chicken, spring mix, apples, raisins, mushrooms, green onions and pecans in a large salad bowl. Add the desired amount of dressing and mix well. Serve immediately.

Serves 6 to 8

Strawberry Spinach Salad

Caramelized Pecans
1/4 to 1/2 cup (1/2 to 1 stick) butter
1 cup sugar
1 1/2 cups pecan halves

Poppy Seed Dressing
1 1/2 to 2 cups vegetable oil
2/3 cup vinegar
1/2 cup sugar
1/4 cup poppy seeds

3 or 4 green onions, chopped
2 teaspoons dry mustard
2 teaspoons salt

Salad
16 ounces baby spinach leaves, torn
    into bite-size pieces
2 cups thinly sliced celery
1 pint fresh strawberries, sliced

For the pecans, melt the butter in a heavy skillet and add the sugar and pecans. Cook until the pecans are light brown and glazed, stirring constantly. Spread the pecans in a single layer on a baking sheet and let stand until cool. Break up clumps if necessary.

For the dressing, combine the oil, vinegar, sugar, poppy seeds, green onions, dry mustard and salt in a blender and process to the desired consistency. Chill, covered, in the refrigerator.

For the salad, toss the spinach, celery and strawberries in a salad bowl. Drizzle with the vinaigrette and toss to coat. Sprinkle with the pecans and serve immediately.

Serves 6 to 8

Chocolate Lover's Delight Pie

2 cups (12 ounces) milk chocolate morsels
10 large marshmallows
1/4 cup milk
1/8 teaspoon salt
1/2 cup walnuts, finely chopped
1 cup heavy whipping cream, whipped
1 baked (10-inch) graham cracker pie shell

Combine the chocolate morsels, marshmallows, milk and salt in a double boiler over hot water. Cook until blended, stirring frequently. Remove from the heat and let stand until cool.

Stir the walnuts into the chocolate mixture and fold in the whipped cream. Spoon the chocolate filling into the pie shell and chill for 2 to 10 hours. Slice and garnish each serving with chocolate shavings.

Serves 8

Chocolate Sherry Cream Bars

Chocolate Crust

    1 cup all-purpose flour
    1/4 teaspoon salt
    2/3 cup (4 ounces) semisweet
        chocolate chips
    1 cup (2 sticks) butter
    4 eggs
    2 cups sugar
    1 teaspoon vanilla extract

Sherry Filling

    4 cups confectioners' sugar
    1/2 cup (1 stick) butter, softened
    1/4 cup heavy cream
    1/4 cup sherry
    1 cup walnuts, chopped

Chocolate Topping

    2 cups (12 ounces) semisweet
        chocolate chips
    6 tablespoons water
    1/2 cup (1 stick) butter

For the crust, preheat the oven to 325 degrees. Sift the flour and salt together. Combine the chocolate chips and butter in a microwave-safe bowl. Microwave until blended and stir. Cool slightly. Beat the eggs in a mixing bowl until pale yellow. Add the sugar gradually, beating constantly until blended. Stir in the vanilla. Combine the chocolate mixture, flour mixture and egg mixture in a mixing bowl and beat for 1 minute. Pour into a greased and lightly floured 10×14-inch baking pan or 11×17-inch baking pan for thinner bars and bake for 25 minutes. Let stand until cool.

For the filling, beat the confectioners' sugar and butter in a mixing bowl until creamy. Add the cream and sherry gradually, beating constantly until light and fluffy. Stir in the walnuts. Spread the filling over the baked layer and chill in the refrigerator.

For the topping, combine the chocolate chips, water and butter in a microwave-safe bowl and microwave until blended, stirring occasionally. Spread the topping over the chilled layers. Let stand until set and cut into bars.

Makes 3 to 4 dozen bars

Summer Trifle

Custard

1 cup sugar
1/4 cup cornstarch
1/2 teaspoon salt
2 eggs, lightly beaten
4 cups milk
1 tablespoon vanilla extract

Trifle

1 angel food cake, cut into
    1/2-inch slices
1 (16-ounce) package frozen
    raspberries in syrup, thawed
1/2 cup orange juice
16 ounces fresh blackberries,
    sweetened, or frozen raspberries
Sweetened whipped cream

For the custard, mix 1/2 cup of the sugar, 2 tablespoons of the cornstarch and 1/4 teaspoon of the salt in a nonstick saucepan and stir in one of the eggs. Add 2 cups of the milk gradually, whisking constantly until blended. Bring to a boil over medium heat, stirring constantly. Remove from the heat and let stand until warm. Stir in 1 1/2 teaspoons of the vanilla. Repeat the process with the remaining sugar, remaining cornstarch, remaining salt, remaining egg, remaining milk and remaining vanilla.

For the trifle, line the bottom of a footed trifle dish with one-third of the cake slices. Sprinkle with the undrained raspberries and spread with the first batch of the warm custard. Layer with half the remaining cake slices and drizzle with half the orange juice. Sprinkle generously with sweetened blackberries. Pour the remaining batch of warm custard over the prepared layers. Top with the remaining cake slices and drizzle with the remaining orange juice. Chill, covered with plastic wrap, for 8 to 10 hours. Just before serving spread with 1 to 1 1/2 inches of sweetened whipped cream.

Serves 6 to 8

Sangria

3 1/2 cups dry red wine
1/2 cup fresh lemon juice
1/2 cup orange juice
1/2 cup sugar

1/4 cup brandy
1 1/4 cups sparkling water, chilled
1 lemon, thinly sliced
1 orange, thinly sliced

Mix the wine, lemon juice, orange juice, sugar and brandy in a glass pitcher and chill for several hours. Stir in the sparkling water, lemon slices and orange slices just before serving. Pour over ice in glasses.

Serves 6

Fall Lunch Menu

 ◆ Peppery Pumpkin Soup
 ◆ Roasted Teriyaki Beef Tenderloin
 ◆ Baked Cauliflower
 ◆ Spinach Salad with Gorgonzola
 ◆ Orzo Salad with Sun-Dried Tomatoes and Kalamata Olives
 ◆ Romaine Salad with Hearts of Palm and Artichokes
 ◆ Lasagna with Artichokes and Béchamel Sauce
 ◆ Chocolate Peanut Treats
 ◆ Great Pumpkin Cookies
 ◆ Espresso Brownies
 ◆ Apple Streusel Pie

Peppery Pumpkin Soup

2 (16-ounce) cans pumpkin purée
2¹/4 cups chicken broth
¹/2 teaspoon salt
¹/2 teaspoon onion powder
¹/2 teaspoon freshly ground pepper

¹/4 teaspoon ground nutmeg
3 cups half-and-half
¹/2 cup sour cream
1 tablespoon unsalted pumpkin seeds

Combine the pumpkin, broth, salt, onion powder, pepper and nutmeg in a medium saucepan and mix well. Cook over medium heat for 10 minutes or until bubbly, stirring occasionally. Stir in the half-and-half and cook over low heat for 5 minutes, stirring occasionally; do not boil. Ladle into soup bowls. Top each serving with a dollop of sour cream and sprinkle with the pumpkin seeds.

Serves 8

Roasted Teriyaki Beef Tenderloin

2 pounds beef tenderloin
1 cup sherry
1 cup soy sauce
2 tablespoons dry onion soup mix
2 tablespoons brown sugar
2 tablespoons water

Place the tenderloin in a large sealable plastic bag. Mix the sherry, soy sauce, soup mix and brown sugar in a bowl. Reserve ¹/2 cup of the sherry mixture. Pour the remaining sherry mixture over the tenderloin and seal tightly. Turn to coat. Marinate in the refrigerator for 8 to 10 hours, turning occasionally.

Preheat the oven to 450 degrees. Remove the tenderloin from the plastic bag and arrange in a roasting pan. Roast for 40 to 50 minutes or to the desired degree of doneness. Let rest for 10 minutes and thinly slice. Heat the reserved sherry mixture and water in a small saucepan and drizzle over the tenderloin on a platter.

Serves 8

Baked Cauliflower

Florets of 1 head cauliflower
1 cup sour cream
1 cup (4 ounces) shredded Monterey Jack cheese
1/4 cup mayonnaise
1/4 cup dry white wine
1 tablespoon chopped fresh Italian parsley
2 teaspoons rinsed drained capers
1/2 teaspoon kosher salt
1/4 cup (1 ounce) grated Parmesan cheese
Paprika to taste

Preheat the oven to 350 degrees. Steam the cauliflower for 6 to 8 minutes or until tender. Combine the sour cream, Monterey Jack cheese, mayonnaise, wine, parsley, capers and kosher salt in a bowl and mix well. Fold in the cauliflower and spoon the cauliflower mixture into a buttered 9×13-inch baking dish. Sprinkle with the Parmesan cheese and paprika and bake for 20 minutes.

Serves 6 to 8

Spinach Salad with Gorgonzola

12 ounces baby spinach, torn
1 cup crumbled Gorgonzola cheese
1 cup pecan pieces, toasted
1/2 cup dried cranberries
3 tablespoons olive oil
1 tablespoon balsamic vinegar
1/2 teaspoon grated lemon zest
Salt and pepper to taste

Toss the spinach, cheese, pecans and cranberries in a large salad bowl. Combine the olive oil, vinegar, lemon zest, salt and pepper in a jar with a tight-fitting lid and seal tightly. Shake to mix. Drizzle the vinaigrette over the spinach mixture and mix until coated. Serve immediately.

Serves 6

Orzo Salad with Sun-Dried Tomatoes and Kalamata Olives

Dijon Vinaigrette
- 1/4 cup fresh lemon juice
- 1 tablespoon minced shallot
- 1 tablespoon white wine vinegar
- 2 teaspoons Dijon mustard
- 1 teaspoon kosher salt
- 1 teaspoon freshly ground pepper
- 1/2 cup olive oil

Salad
- 1 pound asparagus, blanched
- 16 ounces orzo
- 1/4 cup olive oil
- 8 ounces cremini mushrooms, sliced

- 3 tablespoons chopped shallots
- 2 tablespoons minced garlic
- 1 cup drained oil-pack sun-dried tomatoes, julienned
- 1 small red bell pepper, thinly sliced
- 6 green onions, thinly sliced
- 6 ounces feta cheese, crumbled
- 1/2 cup fresh mint, coarsely chopped
- 1/2 cup (2 ounces) freshly grated Parmesan cheese
- 1/2 cup sliced kalamata olives
- 1/2 cup fresh basil, thinly sliced
- Salt and pepper to taste
- 1 cup pine nuts, toasted

For the vinaigrette, whisk the lemon juice, shallot, vinegar, Dijon mustard, salt and pepper in a bowl until combined. Add the olive oil gradually, whisking constantly until the olive oil is incorporated.

For the salad, slice the asparagus spears diagonally into 1-inch pieces. Cook the pasta using the package directions until al dente and drain. Toss the pasta with 2 tablespoons of the olive oil in a bowl and cool to room temperature. Heat the remaining 2 tablespoons olive oil in a large heavy skillet over medium-high heat. Add the mushrooms and sauté for 2 minutes. Reduce the heat to medium and stir in the shallots and garlic. Sauté for 5 minutes. Toss the mushroom mixture with the pasta.

Add the asparagus, sun-dried tomatoes, bell pepper, green onions, feta cheese, mint, Parmesan cheese, olives and basil to the pasta mixture and mix gently. Add the vinaigrette and toss until coated. Season with salt and pepper and sprinkle with the pine nuts. Garnish with teardrop or pear tomatoes and sprigs of Italian parsley. Serve at room temperature. You may prepare up to 1 day in advance and store, covered, in the refrigerator. Bring to room temperature before serving.

Serves 8 or more

Romaine Salad with Hearts of Palm and Artichokes

Sun-Dried Tomato Vinaigrette
1/2 cup olive oil
1/4 cup red wine vinegar
1/4 cup drained oil-pack sun-dried tomatoes, finely chopped
1 teaspoon minced fresh garlic
1 teaspoon ground sumac
1 teaspoon freshly ground pepper
Salt to taste

Salad
1 (14-ounce) can artichoke hearts, drained and patted dry
1 (14-ounce) can hearts of palm, drained and patted dry
7 cups coarsely chopped romaine
1 small red onion, thinly sliced
1/2 cup fresh Italian parsley, coarsely chopped
12 ounces cherry tomatoes, cut into halves
Salt and pepper to taste
1 ounce Parmesan cheese, shaved

For the vinaigrette, combine the olive oil, vinegar, sun-dried tomatoes, garlic, sumac, pepper and salt in a jar with a tight-fitting lid and seal tightly. Shake to mix.

For the salad, cut the artichokes into quarters and cut the hearts of palm diagonally into 1/2-inch slices. Combine the artichokes, hearts of palm, romaine, onion and parsley in a large bowl and mix well. Chill, covered, in the refrigerator until cold. Add the tomatoes and vinaigrette and toss to coat. Season with salt and pepper and sprinkle with the cheese. Serve immediately. Add kalamata olives, sliced radishes and/or crumbled feta cheese, if desired. You may substitute one 10-ounce package drained, thawed frozen artichokes for the canned artichokes.

Serves 6 to 8

Lasagna with Artichokes and Béchamel Sauce

Béchamel Sauce
- 5 tablespoons butter
- 5 tablespoons all-purpose flour
- 1 1/2 cups half-and-half
- 1 cup chicken broth
- 1/4 teaspoon salt
- 1/4 teaspoon ground nutmeg
- 1/8 teaspoon white pepper

Lasagna
- 1 pound sweet Italian sausage, casings removed and sausage crumbled
- 2 tablespoons olive oil
- 2 cups sliced stemmed shiitake mushrooms (about 3 1/2 ounces)
- 1 cup chopped yellow onion
- 3 garlic cloves, minced
- 1 (12-ounce) jar roasted red peppers, drained and julienned
- 1 (14-ounce) can artichoke hearts, drained and cut into 1/2-inch pieces
- 1/2 cup fresh basil, chopped
- Salt and pepper to taste
- 14 lasagna noodles
- 1 pound whole milk mozzarella cheese, shredded
- 1 cup (4 ounces) freshly grated Parmesan cheese

For the sauce, melt the butter in a medium saucepan over medium-high heat. Stir in the flour. Cook for 3 minutes or until thick and golden brown in color, stirring constantly. Add the half-and-half and broth all at once, whisking constantly until blended.

Cook over medium heat for 5 minutes or until the mixture comes to a boil, stirring constantly. Reduce the heat to low and simmer for 2 minutes. Stir in the salt, nutmeg and white pepper. Remove from the heat and press a sheet of waxed paper over the surface of the sauce to prevent a film from forming.

For the lasagna, brown the sausage in a skillet over medium heat for 8 minutes and drain. Remove the sausage to paper towels to drain completely. Wipe the skillet with a paper towel. Heat the olive oil in the skillet and add the mushrooms, onion and garlic. Sauté for 5 minutes or until the onion is tender. Stir in the sausage, roasted peppers, artichokes and basil. Season with salt and pepper.

Preheat the oven to 350 degrees. Spread 1/2 cup of the sauce over the bottom of a 9×13-inch baking dish sprayed with nonstick cooking spray. Layer with enough of the noodles to cover. Top with some of the sausage mixture, some of the mozzarella cheese and some of the Parmesan cheese. Continue the layering process with one-half of the remaining sauce, one-half of the remaining noodles, the remaining sausage mixture, one-half of the remaining mozzarella cheese and one-half of the remaining Parmesan cheese. Continue the layering process with the remaining sauce, remaining noodles, remaining mozzarella cheese and the remaining Parmesan cheese. Bake for 40 to 45 minutes or until bubbly and light brown. Let stand for 5 to 10 minutes before serving.

Serves 8

Chocolate Peanut Treats

2 cups (12 ounces) semisweet
  chocolate chips
2 cups (12 ounces) butterscotch chips
1 (18-ounce) jar creamy peanut butter
1 cup (2 sticks) butter
1 (5-ounce) can evaporated milk

1/4 cup vanilla pudding and pie
  filling mix
2 (1-pound) packages
  confectioners' sugar
1 pound salted peanuts

Combine the chocolate chips and butterscotch chips in a double boiler over simmering water. Cook until blended, stirring frequently. Add the peanut butter and stir until smooth. Spread half the chocolate chip mixture in a greased 10×15-inch baking pan. Chill until firm.

Bring the butter, evaporated milk and pudding mix to a boil in a saucepan. Cook for 2 minutes, stirring constantly. Remove from the heat and beat in the confectioners' sugar until smooth. Spread over the chilled layer. Stir the peanuts into the remaining chocolate chip mixture and spread over the prepared layers. Chill until firm and cut into 2-inch squares.

Makes 30 (2-inch-square) pieces

Great Pumpkin Cookies

2 cups all-purpose flour
1 cup quick-cooking oats or rolled oats
1 teaspoon baking soda
1 teaspoon salt
1 teaspoon ground cinnamon
1 cup (2 sticks) butter

1 cup granulated sugar
1 cup packed brown sugar
1 teaspoon vanilla extract
1 egg, lightly beaten
1 cup solid-pack pumpkin

Preheat the oven to 350 degrees. Mix the flour, oats, baking soda, salt and cinnamon in a bowl. Beat the butter in a mixing bowl until creamy, scraping the bowl occasionally. Add the granulated sugar and brown sugar gradually, beating constantly until light and fluffy. Mix in the vanilla and egg. Add the flour mixture alternately with the pumpkin, mixing well after each addition.

Drop the dough by 1/4 cupfuls 2 inches apart onto a lightly greased cookie sheet. Spread the dough into pumpkin shapes, adding additional dough to form stems. Bake for 15 to 20 minutes or until light brown. Cool on the cookie sheet for 2 minutes and remove to a wire rack to cool completely. Frost, if desired, with traditional pumpkin colors. Store in an airtight container. You may drop the dough by teaspoonfuls. Add semisweet chocolate chips, raisins and/or nuts for variety.

Makes 19 or 20 cookies

Espresso Brownies

2 ounces unsweetened chocolate,
   chopped
1/2 cup (1 stick) butter
3 tablespoons instant espresso powder
1 cup sugar

2 eggs
1/2 teaspoon vanilla extract
1/4 teaspoon salt
1/4 cup all-purpose flour
1 cup walnuts, chopped

Preheat the oven to 325 degrees. Combine the chocolate and butter in a microwave-safe bowl. Microwave until blended, stirring occasionally. Add the espresso powder and stir until dissolved.

Combine the chocolate mixture, sugar, eggs, vanilla and salt in a mixing bowl and beat vigorously until blended. Add the flour and beat just until combined. Stir in the walnuts. Spread the batter in a buttered and floured 8×8-inch baking pan and bake for 25 to 30 minutes or until the edges pull from the sides of the pan. Cool in the pan on a wire rack for 15 minutes. Cut into squares and cool completely on the wire rack. Store in an airtight container.

Makes 16 brownies

Apple Streusel Pie

Streusel Topping
1/2 cup packed brown sugar
1/3 cup all-purpose flour
1/4 cup (1/2 stick) butter
1/4 teaspoon ground cinnamon
1/4 cup chopped pecans

Apple Pie
1/4 cup chopped pecans
1 unbaked (9-inch) pie shell
1 cup sugar
2 tablespoons all-purpose flour
1/2 teaspoon ground cinnamon
1/4 teaspoon ground nutmeg
6 cups thinly sliced tart apples
2 tablespoons butter

For the topping, combine the brown sugar, flour, butter and cinnamon in a bowl and stir with a fork until crumbly. Stir in the pecans.

For the pie, preheat the oven to 425 degrees. Sprinkle the pecans over the bottom of the pie shell. Mix the sugar, flour, cinnamon and nutmeg in a bowl. Add the apples to the sugar mixture and toss to coat. Mound the apple mixture in the prepared pie shell and dot with the butter. Spread the topping evenly over the top of the pie and bake for 10 minutes. Reduce the oven temperature to 350 degrees and bake for 40 minutes longer, checking after 30 minutes and covering with foil if needed to prevent the topping from overbrowning.

Serves 6 to 8

Winter Lunch Menu

◆ Hot Crab Dip

◆ Meatballs with Sweet-and-Sour Sauce

◆ Smoked Salmon Pâté

◆ Pot Roast

◆ Roast Beef Salad

◆ Braised Chicken over Fettuccini

◆ Pasta Salad with Brie

◆ Romaine Salad with Two Cheeses

◆ Refrigerator Rolls

◆ Cheesecake

◆ Almond Crunch Cookies

◆ Pecan Squares

Hot Crab Dip

8 ounces cream cheese, softened
6 ounces crab meat, shells and cartilage removed
2 or 3 green onions, sliced
Dash of Tabasco sauce
Sliced almonds

Preheat the oven to 350 degrees. Combine the cream cheese, crab meat, green onions and Tabasco sauce in a bowl and mix until combined. Spoon the crab mixture into a small baking dish and bake for 25 minutes. Sprinkle with the almonds and bake for 10 minutes longer. Serve with chips and/or assorted party crackers. You may prepare up to 4 hours in advance and store, covered, in the refrigerator. Bake just before serving as directed above.

Makes 1 1/2 cups

Meatballs with Sweet-and-Sour Sauce

2 cups undrained sauerkraut
1 (16-ounce) can whole cranberry sauce (2 cups)
1 1/4 cups chili sauce
1 1/4 cups water
1 cup packed brown sugar
3 pounds frozen cooked meatballs (do not thaw)

Combine the sauerkraut, cranberry sauce, chili sauce, water and brown sugar in a slow cooker and mix well. Add the frozen meatballs and cook on Low for 2 to 3 hours or longer. You may bake in a 9×13-inch baking dish at 350 degrees for 40 minutes.

Serves 8

Smoked Salmon Pâté

2 (7-ounce) cans smoked salmon, or 1
   pound hot smoked salmon
1 cup (2 sticks) butter, melted
1 cup sour cream

1/4 cup fresh lemon juice
2 teaspoons dried dill weed
Salt and pepper to taste

Combine the salmon, butter, sour cream, lemon juice, dill weed, salt and pepper in a mixing bowl and beat until combined. Chill, covered, for 8 to 10 hours. Bring to room temperature and garnish with lemon slices. Serve with seasoned crackers. You may store, covered, in the refrigerator for up to 2 days.

Makes 3 cups

Pot Roast

1/2 cup all-purpose flour
1/2 teaspoon salt
1/2 teaspoon freshly ground pepper
1 (3- to 4-pound) chuck roast
   with bone
1/4 cup (or more) olive oil
13/4 cups beef stock

6 red potatoes, cut into halves
3 onions, cut into quarters
4 carrots, cut into halves
2 fennel bulbs, cut into quarters
1 cup sherry
4 garlic cloves, chopped
11/2 teaspoons dry mustard

Preheat the oven to 300 degrees. Mix the flour, salt and pepper in a sealable plastic bag and add the roast. Seal tightly and shake to coat. Remove the roast from the bag and brush off the excess flour mixture. Reserve the flour mixture remaining in the bag.

Heat the olive oil in a Dutch oven over medium heat. Add the roast and cook until brown on all sides, turning occasionally. Remove the roast to a platter, reserving the pan drippings. Bring the reserved pan drippings, and additional olive oil (up to 1/4 cup) if desired, to a boil and stir in the reserved flour mixture. Cook until thickened, stirring constantly. Add the stock and water if needed and mix well. Return the roast and any accumulated juices to the pan. Add the potatoes, onions, carrots, fennel, sherry, garlic and dry mustard and mix well. Bake, covered, for 3 to 4 hours, stirring occasionally. Double the recipe for a large crowd.

Serves 6

Roast Beef Salad

Blue Cheese Dressing
1/2 cup olive oil or vegetable oil
1/4 cup red wine vinegar
3 tablespoons crumbled blue cheese
2 tablespoons finely chopped fresh parsley or cilantro
2 teaspoons Dijon mustard
1 garlic clove, crushed
1/2 teaspoon sugar
Salt and pepper to taste

Salad
1 1/2 pounds chilled roast beef, julienned
12 small fresh mushrooms, sliced
12 cherry tomatoes, cut into halves
1 (14-ounce) can artichoke hearts, drained and chopped
1 avocado, sliced

For the dressing, combine the olive oil, vinegar, cheese, parsley, Dijon mustard, garlic, sugar, salt and pepper in a jar with a tight-fitting lid and seal tightly. Shake to combine. Chill in the refrigerator. Substitute Gorgonzola cheese for the blue cheese for a milder flavor.

For the salad, toss the roast beef, mushrooms, tomatoes, artichokes and avocado in a large salad bowl. Add the dressing and mix until coated. You may serve on a bed of lettuce.

Serves 6

Braised Chicken over Fettuccini

2 pounds boneless skinless
   chicken thighs
1/2 teaspoon salt
1/2 teaspoon freshly ground pepper
1/4 cup olive oil
2 yellow onions, thinly sliced
4 garlic cloves, thinly sliced
1/2 cup dry white wine
2*1/2* cups no-added-salt chicken broth
1 teaspoon chopped fresh thyme
1/2 teaspoon chopped fresh rosemary

1 bay leaf
1/2 teaspoon whole fennel seeds
3 whole cloves
1/2 teaspoon salt
1/2 teaspoon freshly ground pepper
1 pound fettuccini, cooked al dente
   and drained
Freshly grated Parmesan cheese
Chopped fresh Italian parsley or
   mixed fresh herbs of choice
   (basil, thyme, marjoram)

Preheat the oven to 325 degrees. Season the chicken with 1/2 teaspoon salt and 1/2 teaspoon pepper. Heat the olive oil in a Dutch oven over medium-high heat. Add the chicken in batches to the hot oil and cook until brown on both sides, turning occasionally. Remove the chicken to a platter, reserving the pan drippings.

Add the onions and garlic to the reserved pan drippings and cook over medium heat until the onions are tender and the garlic begins to turn golden brown, stirring frequently. Stir in the wine and cook for 2 minutes, scraping the bottom of the pan to dislodge any browned bits. Add the broth, thyme, rosemary, bay leaf, fennel seeds, cloves, 1/2 teaspoon salt and 1/2 teaspoon pepper and mix well. Return the chicken and any accumulated juices to the pan and bring to a simmer.

Bake, covered, for 1 hour or until the chicken is tender. Discard the bay leaf and cloves. If the sauce appears too thin, remove the chicken to a heated platter and cover to keep warm. Boil the sauce gently until slightly thickened and return the chicken to the pan. Arrange the warm pasta on a platter and spoon the chicken and sauce over the pasta. Sprinkle with cheese and parsley and serve immediately.

Serves 8

Pasta Salad with Brie

1 pound tomatoes, chopped
1 pound Brie cheese, rind removed and cheese chopped
1 cup fresh basil, julienned
3 or 4 garlic cloves, minced
3/4 to 1 cup olive oil
2 teaspoons salt
1 teaspoon freshly ground pepper
1 1/2 pounds penne
Salt to taste
1 cup (4 ounces) grated Parmesan cheese, or to taste

Combine the tomatoes, Brie cheese, basil, garlic, olive oil, 2 teaspoons salt and the pepper in a large nonreactive bowl and mix well. Let stand, covered with plastic wrap, at room temperature for 4 to 10 hours.

Cook the pasta in salted water using the package directions and drain. Add the hot pasta to the tomato mixture and toss until the Brie cheese melts. Stir in the Parmesan cheese and serve at room temperature. The salt is essential for the taste.

Serves 8

Romaine Salad with Two Cheeses

3/4 cup olive oil
1/2 cup (2 ounces) shredded Parmesan cheese
1/4 cup (1 ounce) shredded Romano cheese
2 avocados, chopped
6 green onions, chopped
Juice of 2 lemons
2 teaspoons Beau Monde seasoning
1/4 teaspoon salt
2 heads romaine, trimmed and torn into bite-size pieces

Combine the olive oil, Parmesan cheese, Romano cheese, avocados, green onions, lemon juice, Beau Monde seasoning and salt in a large bowl and mix well. Arrange the romaine over the top; do not mix. Chill, covered, for 4 to 24 hours. Toss just before serving.

Serves 6 to 8

Refrigerator Rolls

2 envelopes dry yeast
1/4 cup lukewarm water
2 cups milk
1 cup (2 sticks) butter

4 eggs
3/4 cup sugar
2 teaspoons salt
7 cups all-purpose flour

Dissolve the yeast in the lukewarm water in a bowl. Let stand for 10 to 15 minutes. Scald the milk in a saucepan. Add the butter to the hot milk and stir until melted. Beat the eggs in a mixing bowl until blended. Beat in the sugar and salt. Add the milk mixture and beat until combined. Add the yeast mixture and flour and beat until a dough forms.

Turn the dough onto a lightly floured surface and knead several times. Do not allow the dough to become too stiff. Place the dough in a greased bowl, turning to coat the surface. Chill, covered, for 2 to 10 hours. Shape the dough as desired and arrange on a baking sheet. Let rise until doubled in bulk. Preheat the oven to 350 degrees and bake for 15 to 20 minutes or until light brown. Decrease the sugar to 2/3 cup for a less sweet dough.

Makes about 2 dozen rolls depending on shape

Cheesecake

Graham Cracker Crust
   13 graham crackers, finely crushed
   1/2 cup (1 stick) butter, melted

Cream Cheese Filling
   16 ounces cream cheese, softened
   2/3 cup sugar
   2 eggs, beaten

2 teaspoons vanilla extract
1 teaspoon fresh lemon juice

Sour Cream Topping
1 1/2 cups sour cream
3 1/2 tablespoons sugar
1 teaspoon fresh lemon juice
1 teaspoon vanilla extract

For the crust, preheat the oven to 325 degrees. Mix the graham cracker crumbs and butter in a bowl and pat the crumb mixture over the bottom and up the side of a 9-inch springform pan. Bake for 10 minutes. Maintain the oven temperature.

For the filling, combine the cream cheese, sugar, eggs, vanilla and lemon juice in a mixing bowl. Beat with a mixer fitted with a paddle attachment until blended, scraping the bowl occasionally. Spread the cream cheese mixture over the baked layer and bake for 25 minutes. Reduce the oven temperature to 300 degrees.

For the topping, combine the sour cream, sugar, lemon juice and vanilla in a bowl and mix well. Spread the sour cream mixture over the baked layers and bake for 10 minutes. Cool in the pan on a wire rack. Chill, covered, for 8 to 10 hours before serving.

Serves 12

Almond Crunch Cookies

3 1/2 cups all-purpose flour
1 cup whole wheat flour
1 teaspoon baking soda
1 teaspoon cream of tartar
1 teaspoon salt
1 cup granulated sugar
1 cup confectioners' sugar
1 cup (2 sticks) butter, softened
1 cup vegetable oil
2 eggs
1/4 teaspoon almond extract (optional)
2 cups almonds, coarsely chopped
1 (6-ounce) package almond brickle

Preheat the oven to 350 degrees. Mix the all-purpose flour, whole wheat flour, baking soda, cream of tartar and salt in a bowl. Combine the granulated sugar, confectioners' sugar, butter and oil in a mixing bowl and beat until creamy, scraping the bowl occasionally. Add the eggs and flavoring and beat until blended. Beat in the flour mixture until combined. Stir in the almonds and brickle.

Shape the dough by tablespoonfuls into balls and arrange 2 inches apart on an ungreased cookie sheet. Flatten the balls in a crisscross pattern using a fork coated with sugar. Bake for 12 to 18 minutes or until light brown. Cool on the cookie sheet for 5 minutes. Remove to a wire rack to cool completely.

Makes 3 1/2 dozen cookies

Pecan Squares

Brown Sugar Crust

1 cup (2 sticks) plus 2 tablespoons unsalted butter, softened
3/4 cup packed light brown sugar
1/2 teaspoon salt
3 cups all-purpose flour

Pecan Filling

1/2 cup (1 stick) butter
1/2 cup packed light brown sugar
6 tablespoons honey
2 tablespoons granulated sugar
2 tablespoons heavy cream
1/4 teaspoon salt
2 cups pecan halves
1/2 teaspoon vanilla extract

For the crust, combine the butter and brown sugar in a mixing bowl. Beat at medium speed using a mixer fitted with a paddle attachment for 2 minutes or until light and fluffy. Add the salt and beat until blended. Add the flour 1 cup at a time, beating constantly until fully incorporated after each addition. Continue beating until the dough begins to form large clumps.

Press the dough 1/4 inch thick over the bottom of a 9×13-inch baking pan and prick with a fork. Chill for 20 minutes or until firm. Preheat the oven to 375 degrees and bake for 18 to 20 minutes or until golden brown. Cool in the pan on a wire rack. Reduce the oven temperature to 325 degrees.

For the filling, combine the butter, brown sugar, honey, granulated sugar, cream and salt in a medium saucepan. Bring to a boil over high heat and boil for 1 minute or until the mixture coats the back of a spoon, stirring constantly. Remove from the heat and stir in the pecans and vanilla.

Pour the filling over the cooled crust and bake for 15 to 20 minutes or until bubbly. Remove to a wire rack to cool. Run a sharp knife around the edges of the pan and invert onto the wire rack. Then invert onto a cutting board, filling side up. Cut into squares. Store in an airtight container for up to 1 week.

Makes 32 squares

Spring Lunch Menu

◆ Green Salad with Shrimp

◆ Mediterranean Pasta Salad with Basil

◆ Chicken Salad Pie

◆ Grilled Potato Salad with Mandarin Oranges and Rosemary

◆ Muffinettes Supreme

◆ Chocolate Chip Banana Nut Bread

◆ Lemon Rub Pie

◆ Lemoncello (Liquore al Limone)

Green Salad with Shrimp

2 cups vegetable oil
1 cup cottage cheese
1/2 onion, chopped
1/2 cup plus 2 tablespoons white vinegar
Juice of 1 lemon
1 garlic clove, minced
1 teaspoon peppercorns
1/4 teaspoon ground cayenne pepper
2 or 3 avocados, sliced
2 pounds small shrimp, cooked and peeled
1 bunch spinach, trimmed
1 head romaine, trimmed and leaves separated
1 head iceberg lettuce, trimmed and leaves separated
1 pound bacon, crisp-cooked and crumbled

Combine the oil, cottage cheese, onion, vinegar, lemon juice, garlic, peppercorns and cayenne pepper in a blender or food processor and process until mixed. Combine the cottage cheese mixture, avocados and shrimp in a bowl and mix gently. Chill, covered, for 8 to 10 hours. Rinse the spinach, romaine and iceberg lettuce and wrap in damp clean kitchen towels. Chill for 8 to 10 hours.

Tear the greens into bite-size pieces. Combine the greens and the shrimp mixture in a salad bowl and mix gently. Sprinkle with the bacon and serve immediately.

Serves 8 to 10

Mediterranean Pasta Salad with Basil

Basil Vinaigrette
  2 tablespoons white wine vinegar or fresh lemon juice
  2 tablespoons chopped fresh basil
  2 garlic cloves, crushed
  1/2 teaspoon Dijon mustard
  Salt and freshly ground pepper to taste
  6 tablespoons extra-virgin olive oil

Salad
  2 cups fusilli or penne
  6 ounces haricots verts, trimmed
  Salt to taste
  2 large tomatoes, chopped, or small grape tomatoes
  Sliced kalamata olives
  2 cups fresh basil leaves, stacked and thinly sliced
  1 (7-ounce) can oil-pack tuna, drained and flaked
  2 hard-cooked eggs, sliced or chopped
  Capers, drained and rinsed

For the vinaigrette, whisk the vinegar, basil, garlic, Dijon mustard, salt and pepper in a bowl until combined. Add the olive oil gradually, whisking constantly until the olive oil is incorporated.

For the salad, cook the pasta using the package directions and drain. Toss the hot pasta with a small amount of the vinaigrette in a bowl. Blanch the green beans in a small amount of boiling salted water in a saucepan until tender-crisp and drain. Immediately plunge into a bowl of ice water to stop the cooking process and drain.

Layer the pasta, tomatoes, olives, basil, green beans and tuna in a large salad bowl, drizzling each layer with some of the vinaigrette. Toss lightly and top with the hard-cooked eggs and capers.

Serves 4

Chicken Salad Pie

1 1/2 cups chopped cooked chicken
1 (9-ounce) can pineapple tidbits,
 drained
1 (8-ounce) can mandarin oranges,
 drained
1/2 to 1 cup walnuts, chopped

1/2 cup chopped celery
1 cup sour cream
2/3 cup mayonnaise
1 baked (9-inch) pie shell
1 cup (4 ounces) shredded
 Cheddar cheese

Combine the chicken, pineapple, mandarin oranges, walnuts and celery in a bowl and mix well. Mix the sour cream and mayonnaise in a bowl and stir the sour cream mixture into the chicken mixture. Spoon the chicken mixture into the pie shell and sprinkle with the cheese. Chill, covered, for 8 to 10 hours.

Serves 8

Grilled Potato Salad with Mandarin Oranges and Rosemary

8 small Yukon Gold or red potatoes
4 to 6 tablespoons (or more) olive oil
1/4 cup steak grill seasoning
1/4 cup chopped fresh rosemary
2 (16-ounce) cans mandarin oranges,
 drained

1/4 cup red wine vinegar, or to taste
1 small red onion, thinly sliced
Salt and freshly ground pepper to taste

Parboil the potatoes in a small amount of boiling water in a saucepan for 10 minutes and drain. Let stand until cool and cut into 1/4-inch slices.

Preheat a cast-iron grill pan until hot. An outdoor grill may be used instead. Toss the potatoes with the olive oil, grill seasoning and rosemary in a large bowl; the olive oil should lightly coat the potatoes. Arrange the potatoes on the hot grill pan and cook for 3 to 5 minutes per side or until grill marks appear. Return the potatoes to the large bowl and cool slightly. Add the mandarin oranges, vinegar and onion and toss gently. Season with salt and pepper. Serve immediately or chill, covered, in the refrigerator. If chilled, bring to room temperature before serving.

Serves 6 to 8

Muffinettes Supreme

1 cup all-purpose flour
1/2 teaspoon baking powder
1/2 teaspoon salt
1 1/2 cups packed brown sugar
4 eggs

1 teaspoon vanilla extract
1 1/2 cups walnuts or pecans,
    finely chopped
1 1/2 cups dates, finely chopped

Preheat the oven to 350 degrees. Sift the flour, baking powder and salt together. Beat the brown sugar, eggs and vanilla in a mixing bowl until blended. Add the flour mixture and beat until smooth. Stir in the walnuts and dates. Chill, covered, for 8 to 10 hours.

Fill miniature muffin cups one-half full and bake for 12 to 15 minutes or until light brown. Serve with cream cheese.

Makes 1 1/2 to 2 dozen muffinettes

Chocolate Chip Banana Nut Bread

1 1/2 cups all-purpose flour
2/3 teaspoon baking soda
1/2 teaspoon salt
1 cup (2 sticks) butter
1 cup sugar
1 cup mashed very ripe bananas
    (2 or 3 bananas)

1/4 cup buttermilk
2 eggs
1 teaspoon vanilla extract
1 cup (6 ounces) semisweet
    chocolate chips
1 cup pecans or walnuts, chopped

Preheat the oven to 350 degrees. Mix the flour, baking soda and salt together. Beat the butter and sugar in a mixing bowl until light and fluffy. Add the bananas, buttermilk, eggs and vanilla and beat until blended. Add the flour mixture and mix just until moistened. Stir in the chocolate chips and pecans.

Spoon the batter evenly into two greased 5×9-inch loaf pans. Bake for 45 to 50 minutes or until a wooden pick inserted in the centers comes out clean. Cool in the pans for 10 minutes and remove to a wire rack to cool completely.

Makes 2 loaves

Lemon Rub Pie

2 cups sugar
1/2 cup (1 stick) butter, softened
5 eggs
2/3 cup fresh lemon juice
3 tablespoons all-purpose flour
1 tablespoon grated lemon zest
1 unbaked (9-inch) pie shell

Preheat the oven to 350 degrees. Cream the sugar and butter in a bowl of a stand mixer. Add the eggs one at a time, beating well after each addition. Add the lemon juice, flour and lemon zest and mix until combined.

Spoon the lemon filling into the pie shell and bake for 30 to 35 minutes or until the top is brown and the filling is set. Cool on a wire rack.

Serves 8

Lemoncello (Liquore al Limone)

15 thick-skin lemons
2 (750-milliliter) bottles 100-proof vodka
4 cups sugar
5 cups water

Scrub the lemons with a vegetable brush and hot water to remove any wax or pesticides. Pat dry with paper towels. Remove the zest in strips with a vegetable peeler, removing any white pith. Combine the lemon zest and 1 bottle of the vodka in a large jar with a tight-fitting lid. Let stand at room temperature in a cool dark environment for 40 days.

After 40 days, mix the sugar and water in a saucepan and bring to a boil. Boil for 5 minutes and remove from the heat. Let stand until cool. Add the syrup and remaining bottle of vodka to the jar containing the vodka and lemon zest.

Let stand, covered, at room temperature in a cool dark environment for 40 more days. Strain the vodka mixture into bottles, discarding the solids. Store in the freezer. Serve ice cold from the freezer in small glasses.

Makes about 2 (750-milliliter) bottles

Mexican Fiesta Menu

+ Cowboy Caviar
+ Mexican Bean Dip with Tortilla Chips
+ Chicken and White Bean Chili
+ Mexican Chicken Casserole
+ Red and Green Rice
+ Nopales Salad
+ Black Bean and White Corn Salad with Ancho Cilantro Vinaigrette
+ Ice Cream with Peach and Raspberry Sauce
+ Lace Cookies

Cowboy Caviar

Red Wine Vinaigrette
1/4 cup extra-virgin olive oil
1/4 cup red wine vinegar
2 garlic cloves, minced
3/4 teaspoon salt, or to taste
1/2 teaspoon freshly ground pepper
1 teaspoon ground cumin
1 teaspoon ground coriander

Dip
1 (15-ounce) can whole kernel corn, drained
1 (14-ounce) can black beans, drained and rinsed
1 (14-ounce) can black-eyed peas, drained and rinsed
1 (14-ounce) can diced tomatoes, drained
2 large avocados, chopped
2/3 cup fresh cilantro, chopped
2/3 cup chopped green onions
1 jalapeño chile, finely chopped

For the vinaigrette, combine the olive oil, vinegar, garlic, salt, pepper, cumin and coriander in a jar with a tight-fitting lid and seal tightly. Shake to mix.

For the dip, mix the corn, beans, peas, tomatoes, avocados, cilantro, green onions and jalapeño chile in a bowl. Add the vinaigrette and toss to coat. Serve with tortilla chips.

Note: Canned chipotle chiles or ground chipotle chile powder to taste may be added. If using canned, start with half a whole chile, finely chopped. If using ground, start with 1/4 teaspoon and let it stand to allow the flavors to meld before adding more. Chipotle adds a wonderful flavor, but use caution as the heat can sneak up on you.

Serves 8 to 10

Mexican Bean Dip

1 (16-ounce) can refried beans
1 cup sour cream
1 tablespoon taco seasoning mix
1 cup (4 ounces) shredded white
    Cheddar cheese
1 cup (4 ounces) shredded Monterey
    Jack cheese
1 tomato, chopped
1 green bell pepper or jalapeño
    chile, chopped
1/2 cup sliced black olives

Preheat the oven to 375 degrees. Spread the beans over the bottom of a 9- or 10-inch quiche dish or pie plate. Mix the sour cream and taco seasoning mix in a bowl and spread over the beans. Sprinkle with the cheeses. Bake for 15 to 20 minutes or until bubbly. Sprinkle with the tomato, bell pepper and olives. Serve with tortilla chips.

Serves 6

Chicken and White Bean Chili

1 tablespoon olive oil
1 cup chopped onion
3 garlic cloves, minced
2 (14-ounce) cans diced tomatoes
2 (14-ounce) cans chicken broth
1 (4-ounce) can chopped green chiles
1 teaspoon dried oregano
1/2 teaspoon ground coriander
1/2 teaspoon ground cumin
3 cups (bite-size pieces) poached chicken
2 (16-ounce) cans Great Northern
    beans, drained and rinsed
3 tablespoons fresh lime juice
1/4 teaspoon freshly ground pepper
2 cups (8 ounces) shredded Cheddar
    cheese
1 (4-ounce) can sliced black olives,
    drained
3 green onions, sliced
1 bunch cilantro, trimmed and chopped
Sour cream

Heat the olive oil in a skillet add the onion and garlic. Sauté until the onion is tender and stir in the undrained tomatoes, broth, green chiles, oregano, coriander and cumin. Bring to a boil and reduce the heat.

Simmer for 20 minutes, stirring occasionally. Stir in the chicken and beans and cook for 15 minutes or until heated through. Stir in the lime juice and pepper. Ladle into chili bowls and top each serving with the cheese, olives, green onions, cilantro and/or sour cream. Serve with tortilla chips or corn bread. Add Tabasco sauce for more zip.

Serves 8 to 10

Mexican Chicken Casserole

4 or 5 whole chicken breasts
Salt and pepper to taste
1 (10-ounce) can cream of mushroom
    soup
1 (10-ounce) can cream of chicken
    soup
1 (7-ounce) can chopped green chiles

8 ounces Cheddar cheese, shredded
1 cup sour cream
1/2 cup chopped onion
1/2 cup milk
3 tablespoons (or more) canned
    chicken broth
12 corn tortillas, torn

Preheat the oven to 350 degrees. Season the chicken with salt and pepper and wrap the pieces individually in foil. Arrange the foil packets on a baking sheet and bake for 1 hour. Remove the chicken from the foil, reserving the broth. Cool slightly and chop the chicken into 1-inch pieces, discarding the skin and bones.

Combine the soups, green chiles, cheese, sour cream, onion, milk, canned broth and reserved broth in a bowl and mix well. Stir in the chicken. Add the tortillas and stir until completely coated. Spoon the chicken mixture into a greased 9×13-inch baking dish and chill, covered, for 8 to 10 hours; remove the cover. Preheat the oven to 350 degrees and bake for 1 1/2 hours.

Serves 6

Red and Green Rice

2 tablespoons olive oil
1 small onion, chopped
2 garlic cloves, minced or crushed
1 1/2 cups long grain rice
3 cups chicken broth
1 (4-ounce) can chopped mild
    green chiles

2 tomatoes, chopped
1 teaspoon chili powder
1/2 teaspoon salt
1/2 teaspoon freshly ground pepper
1/2 cup fresh cilantro, chopped
1/2 cup coarsely chopped pimento-
    stuffed green olives

Heat the olive oil in a 4-quart nonstick saucepan over medium-high heat until hot but not smoking. Sauté the onion and garlic in the hot oil for 2 to 3 minutes or until the onion is tender. Stir in the rice. Cook for 3 minutes or until the rice is golden brown, stirring occasionally. Add the broth, green chiles, tomatoes, chili powder, salt and pepper and mix well. Bring to a boil and reduce the heat.

Simmer, covered, for 25 minutes or just until the rice is tender. Remove from the heat and stir in the cilantro and olives. Let stand, covered, for 10 minutes and fluff with a fork.

Serves 4

Nopales Salad

Sherry Vinaigrette
  1/3 cup sherry vinegar
  2 tablespoons olive oil
  1 tablespoon chopped fresh cilantro
  1 garlic clove, crushed

Salad
  1 1/2 pounds nopales (cactus pads),
    cut into 1-inch-long strips
  2 large tomatoes, chopped
  1 large jalapeño chile, finely chopped
  5 green onions, sliced

For the vinaigrette, combine the vinegar, olive oil, cilantro and garlic in a jar with a tight-fitting lid and seal tightly. Shake to mix.

For the salad, combine the nopales, tomatoes, jalapeño chile and green onions in a bowl and mix well. Add the vinaigrette and toss to coat. Serve immediately.

Serves 6 to 8

Black Bean and White Corn Salad with Ancho Cilantro Vinaigrette

Ancho Cilantro Vinaigrette
  1 dried ancho chile
  1/3 cup seasoned rice vinegar
  1/3 cup fresh lime juice
  1/3 cup olive oil
  1 teaspoon sugar
  1/2 teaspoon salt
  1/2 teaspoon coarsely ground pepper
  1 bunch cilantro, trimmed

Salad
  3 (14-ounce) cans black beans, drained
    and rinsed
  1 (16-ounce) package frozen white
    corn, thawed
  1/2 cup minced red onion
  1/2 cup finely chopped green onions
  2 cups chopped fresh tomatoes

For the vinaigrette, rehydrate the ancho chile in enough water to cover in a bowl for 45 minutes; drain. Discard the seeds from the chile and finely chop. Combine the ancho chile, vinegar, lime juice, olive oil, sugar, salt and pepper in a bowl and mix well. Reserve fifteen to twenty sprigs of the cilantro for garnish. Finely chop enough of the remaining cilantro to measure 1/2 cup and whisk into the vinaigrette.

For the salad, mix the beans, corn, red onion and green onions in a salad bowl. Add the vinaigrette and toss until coated. Fold in the tomatoes and garnish with the reserved cilantro sprigs.

Serves 8 to 10

Peach and Raspberry Sauce

2 tablespoons butter
1/4 cup confectioners' sugar
1/4 cup packed brown sugar
2 tablespoons orange juice
2 tablespoons lemon juice
1 (16-ounce) can freestone peaches, sliced or cut into chunks
1 cup frozen loose-pack raspberries or fresh raspberries
1/4 cup peach brandy

Heat the butter in a saucepan until melted and stir in the confectioners' sugar, brown sugar, orange juice and lemon juice. Bring to a boil and boil until the sugars dissolve, stirring frequently. Stir in the peaches.

Simmer for 5 minutes and gently stir in the raspberries and brandy. Remove from the heat and let stand until room temperature. Drizzle the sauce over ice cream and serve with Lace Cookies. You may prepare in advance and store, covered, in the refrigerator. Bring to room temperature before serving.

Makes 2 1/2 cups

Lace Cookies

2/3 cup packed brown sugar
1/2 cup (1 stick) butter
1/2 cup light corn syrup
1 cup all-purpose flour
1 cup pecans, chopped

Preheat the oven to 350 degrees. Bring the brown sugar, butter and corn syrup to a boil in a saucepan and boil until the sugar dissolves, stirring frequently. Add the flour and pecans and mix until combined.

Drop by teaspoonfuls 5 inches apart onto a cookie sheet lined with baking parchment paper. Bake for 8 to 10 minutes. Immediately roll the warm cookies on a dowel to shape into cones. Let stand until cool and remove from the dowel. Fill with whipped cream, if desired.

Note: If dowels are not available, crushed foil or a clean broomstick may be used.

Makes 15 to 20 cookies

CHRISTMAS LUNCH MENU

◆ Minted Walnuts

◆ Cranberry Relish over Cream Cheese

◆ Orange Shortbread

◆ Stuffed Cornish Game Hens

◆ Roasted Goose with Fruit and Walnut Stuffing

◆ Corn Bread Dressing

◆ Cranberry Conserve

◆ Spinach Mushroom Florentine

◆ Potato Gruyère Galette

◆ Special Chocolate Chip Cookies

◆ Mocha Pecan Truffle Cookies

◆ Apricot-Banana-Cranberry Cake (ABC Cake)

◆ Tumbleweeds

Minted Walnuts

2 cups sugar
3/4 cup evaporated milk
1 tablespoon butter
1/4 teaspoon salt

1 tablespoon peppermint extract
Green food coloring
4 cups walnut halves

Mix the sugar, evaporated milk, butter and salt in the top of a double boiler and place over direct heat. Cook for 2 minutes or until the sugar dissolves, stirring frequently. Reduce the heat and place over simmering water.

Cook for 7 minutes or to 234 to 240 degrees on a candy thermometer, soft-ball stage. Stir in the flavoring and food coloring. Add the walnuts and stir until coated. Spread the walnuts in a single layer on a sheet of foil and let stand until cool. Store in an airtight container.

Makes 4 cups

Cranberry Relish over Cream Cheese

16 ounces cream cheese, softened
2 cups fresh cranberries
3/4 cup sugar
1/3 cup orange juice

1 1/2 tablespoons fresh lemon juice
3/4 teaspoon grated orange zest
1/2 teaspoon grated lemon zest

Beat the cream cheese in a mixing bowl at medium speed until creamy, scraping the bowl occasionally. Spoon the cream cheese into a 2-cup mold lined with plastic wrap. Chill, covered, for 8 hours or longer.

Combine the cranberries, sugar, orange juice, lemon juice, grated orange zest and grated lemon zest in a saucepan and mix well. Bring to a boil over medium heat and boil for 3 to 5 minutes or until the cranberries pop, stirring occasionally. Let stand until cool. Chill, covered, for 8 hours or longer.

Invert the cream cheese onto a serving platter, discarding the plastic wrap. Stir the cranberry relish and spoon over the cream cheese. Garnish with strips of lemon zest and orange zest. Serve with Orange Shortbread on page 187.

Serves 20 to 25

Orange Shortbread

1 cup (2 sticks) butter, softened
3/4 cup confectioners' sugar, sifted
13/4 cups all-purpose flour

1 teaspoon grated orange zest
2 teaspoons thawed frozen orange
 juice concentrate

Preheat the oven to 300 degrees. Beat the butter at medium speed in a mixing bowl until creamy. Add the confectioners' sugar gradually, beating constantly. Add the flour, orange zest and orange juice concentrate and mix well. Spread evenly in a lightly greased 10×15-inch baking pan. Bake for 28 to 30 minutes or until light brown. Remove the pan from the oven and cut the shortbread into rectangles. Cool in the pan on a wire rack. Remove the rectangles from the pan and store in an airtight container for up to 1 week.

Makes 4 dozen

Stuffed Cornish Game Hens

Wild Rice Stuffing
1 cup wild rice
1 (6-ounce) can water chestnuts,
 drained
3/4 cup golden raisins
1/2 cup blanched almonds

Orange Basting Sauce
1 cup orange juice
1/2 cup (1 stick) butter, melted

Apricot Sauce and Assembly
1 cup pineapple apricot jam
2/3 cup vermouth or white wine
2/3 cup fresh or canned apricots,
 chopped
1/4 cup (1/2 stick) butter, melted
4 Cornish game hens

For the stuffing, cook the wild rice using the package directions. Stir in the water chestnuts, raisins and almonds.

For the basting sauce, whisk the orange juice and butter in a bowl until blended.

For the apricot sauce, combine the jam, vermouth, apricots and butter in a saucepan and mix well. Cook until heated through, stirring occasionally. Remove from the heat and cover to keep warm.

To assemble, preheat the oven to 350 degrees. Spoon one-fourth of the stuffing into each game hen and arrange breast side up in a baking pan. Brush with some of the basting sauce and bake for 1 1/4 hours, brushing with the basting sauce throughout the baking process. Spoon one-fourth of the apricot sauce on each of four dinner plates. Slice each game hen lengthwise and arrange one game hen on each prepared plate. Serve immediately.

Serves 4

Roasted Goose with Fruit and Walnut Stuffing

Fruit and Walnut Stuffing
> 1 cup golden raisins
> 3 Golden Delicious apples, peeled and
>   coarsely chopped
> 2 tablespoons fresh lemon juice
> 1 cup walnuts, chopped
> 1 cup cooked wild rice
> 1 teaspoon ground cinnamon
> 1/4 teaspoon ground nutmeg
> 1/2 cup packed brown sugar
> 1/2 cup vermouth or white wine

Apple Basting Sauce
> 2/3 cup vermouth or dry white wine
> 1/2 cup apple jelly
> 1/2 teaspoon ground nutmeg

Goose
> 1 (51/2-pound) goose, dressed
> 1 lemon, cut into quarters
> Salt and pepper to taste
> 1/4 cup bacon drippings, heated
> 4 thick slices bacon

For the stuffing, plump the raisins in enough hot water to generously cover in a bowl; drain. Toss the apples with the lemon juice in a bowl. Add the raisins, walnuts, wild rice, cinnamon, nutmeg, brown sugar and vermouth.

For the sauce, combine the vermouth, jelly and nutmeg in a saucepan and cook until the jelly liquefies, stirring occasionally.

For the goose, preheat the oven to 325 degrees. Rub the outer and inner surfaces of the goose with the lemon quarters and sprinkle with salt and pepper. Spoon the stuffing loosely into the goose cavity and close with skewers.

Arrange the goose breast side up on a rack in a roasting pan. Cover the goose with cheesecloth soaked in the bacon drippings and arrange the bacon over the cheesecloth-covered breast. Roast for 25 minutes per pound or until a meat thermometer registers 180 degrees, basting frequently with the sauce and pan drippings. If the age of the bird is unknown, tenderize by pouring 1 cup of water into the roasting pan and cover the goose during the last hour of the roasting process. Use the pan drippings to prepare gravy, if desired.

Serves 8 to 10

Corn Bread Dressing

6 cups crumbled corn bread
1 apple, chopped
6 ribs celery, chopped
1 onion, chopped
3 large carrots, chopped
4 eggs, lightly beaten
1/4 cup (1/2 stick) butter, melted
2 tablespoons sage
2 tablespoons salt
1 tablespoon pepper
1 jalapeño chile, chopped
Turkey stock or water (optional)

Preheat the oven to 350 degrees. Combine the corn bread, apple, celery, onion, carrots, eggs and butter in a bowl and mix well. Stir in the sage, salt, pepper and jalapeño chile. Add stock if needed for the desired consistency.

Spoon the stuffing into two 5×7-inch loaf pans and bake for 1¼ hours or until the top is brown and cracked. Or, spoon the stuffing into a turkey and bake until the turkey is cooked through.

Serves 10 to 12

Cranberry Conserve

32 ounces fresh cranberries
5 pounds pears, finely chopped
3/4 cup sugar
2/3 cup port
Grated zest of 1 orange

Process the cranberries in a food processor until chopped. Combine the cranberries, pears, sugar, wine and orange zest in a bowl and mix well. Chill, covered, for 24 hours before serving.

Makes 3 cups

Spinach Mushroom Florentine

1 pound cremini mushrooms, sliced
2 (10-ounce) packages frozen chopped
   spinach, thawed and drained
1/4 cup chopped onion
1/4 cup (1/2 stick) butter, melted

1 cup (4 ounces) shredded
   Cheddar cheese
1 teaspoon salt
Garlic powder to taste

Preheat the oven to 350 degrees. Sauté the mushrooms in a nonstick skillet until tender. Cool slightly. Press the excess moisture from the spinach. Combine the spinach, onion, butter, 1/2 cup of the cheese and the salt in a bowl and mix well. Spoon half the spinach mixture into a buttered 9×13-inch baking dish and top with half the mushrooms. Sprinkle with garlic power. Top with the remaining spinach mixture, remaining mushrooms and garlic powder. Sprinkle with the remaining 1/2 cup cheese and bake for 20 minutes or until bubbly.

Serves 6 to 8

Potato Gruyère Galette

3 tablespoons extra-virgin olive oil
8 ounces cremini mushrooms, chopped
1/4 cup minced shallots
Kosher salt and freshly ground pepper
   to taste
1 teaspoon chopped fresh thyme

1 cup (4 ounces) finely grated
   Parmesan cheese
1 cup (4 ounces) finely grated
   Gruyère cheese
3 or 4 Yukon Gold potatoes
1/2 cup cream or milk

Preheat the oven to 350 degrees. Heat the olive oil in a saucepan over medium heat and add the mushrooms and shallots. Sauté for 3 minutes or until tender but not brown. Remove from the heat and season with kosher salt and pepper. Stir in the thyme and let stand until cool. Toss the Parmesan cheese and Gruyère cheese in a bowl.

Coat a 10-inch pie plate or 8×8-inch baking dish with olive oil nonstick cooking spray. Slice the potatoes as thin as possible, discarding the ends. Line the bottom of the prepared pie plate with the potatoes, overlapping in a circle. Top with a 1/4-inch layer of the mushroom mixture and a 1/4-inch layer of the cheese mixture. Repeat the layering process up to three more times using the remaining potatoes, remaining mushroom mixture and remaining cheese mixture. Pour the cream over the prepared layers.

Bake for 30 to 45 minutes or until the potatoes are tender and the top is golden brown and bubbly. Let stand for 10 minutes and cut into wedges or squares. You may cover with foil and let stand at room temperature for 30 minutes before serving.

Serves 6

Special Chocolate Chip Cookies

1¹/2 cups all-purpose flour
1 teaspoon baking soda
1 teaspoon ground cinnamon
¹/2 teaspoon salt
1 cup (2 sticks) butter, softened
1 cup packed brown sugar

¹/2 cup granulated sugar
2 eggs
1 teaspoon vanilla extract
3 cups old-fashioned oats
2 cups (12 ounces) chocolate chips
1 cup walnuts, chopped

Preheat the oven to 350 degrees. Mix the flour, baking soda, cinnamon and salt together. Combine the butter, brown sugar and granulated sugar in a bowl of a stand mixer and beat until creamy, scraping the bowl occasionally. Add the eggs one at a time, mixing well after each addition. Blend in the vanilla. Add the flour mixture and beat until smooth. Mix in the oats and fold in the chocolate chips and walnuts.

Drop by rounded tablespoonfuls onto a nonstick cookie sheet or a cookie sheet lined with baking parchment paper. Bake for 12 minutes or until golden brown. Cool on the cookie sheet for 1 minute and remove to a wire rack to cool completely. Store in an airtight container.

Makes 3 to 4 dozen

Mocha Pecan Truffle Cookies

4 cups all-purpose flour
2/3 cup baking cocoa
1 teaspoon baking powder
¹/2 teaspoon salt
1 cup (2 sticks) butter
1 cup (6 ounces) semisweet
    chocolate pieces

¹/4 cup instant espresso powder
2 cups granulated sugar
2 cups packed brown sugar
5 extra-large eggs
4 teaspoons vanilla extract
2 to 2¹/2 cups pecans, chopped

Preheat the oven to 350 degrees. Mix the flour, baking cocoa, baking powder and salt together. Combine the butter and chocolate pieces in a microwave-safe bowl and microwave until blended; stir. Stir in the espresso powder. Let stand for 5 minutes.

Combine the granulated sugar, brown sugar, eggs and vanilla in a bowl of a stand mixer and beat until creamy, scraping the bowl occasionally. Add the flour mixture gradually, beating constantly. Stir in the espresso mixture and pecans. Drop by rounded teaspoonfuls onto a lightly greased or nonstick cookie sheet. Bake for 10 minutes. Cool on the cookie sheet for 2 minutes and remove to a wire rack to cool completely. Store in an airtight container.

Makes 4 dozen cookies

Apricot-Banana-Cranberry Cake (ABC Cake)

2 1/3 cups all-purpose flour
1 teaspoon baking powder
1 teaspoon baking soda
1/4 teaspoon salt
2 1/2 cups sugar
2 large very ripe bananas, mashed
2 eggs
2 teaspoons vanilla extract
1 cup buttermilk
3/4 cup (1 1/2 sticks) butter, melted
6 ounces dried cranberries
6 ounces dried apricots, chopped
1 1/4 cups walnuts, chopped

Preheat the oven to 350 degrees. Mix the flour, baking powder, baking soda and salt together. Beat the sugar, bananas, eggs and vanilla in a mixing bowl until blended. Add the buttermilk and butter and beat until smooth. Beat in the flour mixture. Fold in the cranberries, apricots and walnuts just until combined.

Spoon the batter into a buttered and floured 12-cup bundt pan and bake for 60 to 70 minutes or until a wooden pick inserted in the center comes out clean. Cool in the pan on a wire rack for 15 minutes. Invert onto the wire rack to cool completely.

Serves 16

Tumbleweeds

2 ounces Kahlúa
1 ounce vodka
1 ounce brandy
4 cups vanilla ice cream

Process the Kahlúa, vodka, brandy and ice cream in a blender until smooth. Pour into chilled Champagne glasses and serve immediately.

Serves 8

APPRECIATION BRUNCH MENU

- Greek Spinach Pie
- John Wayne Eggs
- Breakfast Casserole
- Jets Potatoes
- Granola
- Fruit Salad with Sour Cream and Orange Dressing
- Buttermilk Currant Scones
- Carrot Bread
- Blueberry Muffin Tops
- Luscious Lemon Loaf
- Cranberry Coffee Cake
- Easy Sticky Buns

Greek Spinach Pie

1/2 cup chopped onion
2 tablespoons butter
1 1/2 pounds fresh spinach, trimmed
3 tablespoons butter
3 tablespoons all-purpose flour
1 1/2 cups milk
1 garlic clove, chopped

1 1/2 teaspoons salt
1/4 teaspoon pepper
Dash of ground nutmeg
6 eggs, beaten
8 ounces mozzarella cheese, shredded
1 unbaked (9-inch) pie shell

Preheat the oven to 350 degrees. Sauté the onion in 2 tablespoons butter in a skillet until golden brown. Add the spinach and sauté until wilted. Melt 3 tablespoons butter in a saucepan and stir in the flour. Add the milk gradually, stirring constantly. Cook over low heat until thickened, stirring constantly. Stir in the garlic, salt, pepper and nutmeg. Add to the spinach mixture and mix well. Stir in the eggs and cheese. Pour into the pie shell and bake for 40 to 45 minutes or until firm. Garnish with tomato slices and serve hot.

Note: You may use two 11-ounce packages frozen chopped spinach, thawed and drained, instead of the fresh spinach.

Serves 6

John Wayne Eggs

1 pound Monterey Jack cheese,
    shredded
1 pound Cheddar cheese, shredded
1 (4-ounce) can chopped green chiles
6 egg whites
2/3 cup evaporated milk or
    whipping cream

6 egg yolks
1 tablespoon all-purpose flour
Salt and pepper to taste
2 tomatoes, sliced

Preheat the oven to 325 degrees. Mix the Monterey Jack cheese, Cheddar cheese and green chiles in a bowl and spread the cheese mixture over the bottom of a buttered 9×13-inch baking dish. Beat the egg whites in a mixing bowl until stiff peaks form.

Beat the evaporated milk, egg yolks, flour, salt and pepper in a mixing bowl until blended. Fold the egg whites into the egg yolk mixture and pour over the prepared layer. Use a fork to make sure the milk mixture seeps through the cheese. Bake for 30 minutes and top with the tomatoes. Bake for 15 minutes longer. Serve immediately.

Serves 8

Breakfast Casserole

3 cups frozen hash brown potatoes (do not thaw)
3/4 cup (3 ounces) shredded Monterey Jack cheese
1 cup cooked crumbled hot sausage
1/4 cup chopped green onions
1 (12-ounce) can evaporated milk, or 1 1/4 cups half-and-half
4 eggs
Salt and freshly ground pepper to taste

Layer the frozen potatoes, cheese, sausage and green onions in a buttered 8×8-inch baking dish. Beat the evaporated milk, eggs, salt and pepper in a mixing bowl until blended and pour over the prepared layers. Chill, covered, for 8 to 10 hours.

Remove the cover and place the chilled casserole in a cold oven. Turn the oven to 350 degrees and bake for 1 hour. Serve immediately.

Serves 6

Jets Potatoes

20 ounces frozen hash brown potatoes (do not thaw)
1 cup (4 ounces) shredded Cheddar cheese
2 cups sour cream
1/2 cup milk
4 green onions, chopped
Salt and freshly ground pepper to taste
1/2 cup (2 ounces) shredded Cheddar cheese

Preheat the oven to 350 degrees. Combine the frozen potatoes, 1 cup cheese, the sour cream, milk, green onions, salt and pepper in a bowl and mix well. Spread the potato mixture in a buttered 9×13-inch baking dish and sprinkle with 1/2 cup cheese. Bake for 45 minutes.

Serves 6 to 8

Granola

4½ cups old-fashioned oats
1½ cups shredded coconut
1½ cups pistachios
1½ cups pecans
1½ cups slivered almonds
1½ cups sunflower seeds
¼ teaspoon ground cinnamon

1 cup honey
½ cup packed brown sugar
½ cup molasses
½ cup (1 stick) butter
1 cup finely chopped assorted
    dried fruit (raisins, apricots,
    cranberries, dates)

Preheat the oven to 350 degrees. Mix the oats, coconut, pistachios, pecans, almonds, sunflower seeds and cinnamon in a bowl. Combine the honey, brown sugar, molasses and butter in a saucepan and cook over medium heat until blended, stirring frequently; do not allow to boil.

Pour the honey mixture over the oats mixture and mix until coated. Spread the oats mixture on a greased baking sheet with edges. Bake for 15 minutes or until the oats are golden brown, stirring frequently. Spoon into a heatproof bowl and stir in the dried fruit. Store in airtight containers or sealable plastic bags in a cool environment for up to 2 months. Freeze if storing for longer than 2 months.

Makes 16 to 18 cups

Sour Cream and Orange Dressing

1 cup mayonnaise
1 cup sour cream
3 tablespoons sugar
Juice of 1 orange

2 teaspoons grated orange zest
½ teaspoon ground cinnamon
½ teaspoon ground nutmeg

Combine the mayonnaise, sour cream, sugar, orange juice, orange zest, cinnamon and nutmeg in a bowl and mix well. Serve over assorted fresh fruit. Store leftovers in the refrigerator.

Makes 3 cups

Buttermilk Currant Scones

3 cups all-purpose flour
1/3 cup sugar
2 1/2 teaspoons baking powder
3/4 teaspoon salt
1/2 teaspoon baking soda
3/4 cup (1 1/2 sticks) butter

1 cup buttermilk
3/4 cup currants
1 teaspoon grated orange zest
2 tablespoons sugar
1 tablespoon heavy cream
1/4 teaspoon ground cinnamon

Preheat the oven to 425 degrees. Combine the flour, 1/3 cup sugar, the baking powder, salt and baking soda in a bowl and mix well. Cut in the butter using a pastry blender or two knives until the mixture resembles fresh bread crumbs. Add the buttermilk, currants and orange zest and mix just until moistened. Shape the dough into a ball.

Pat the dough into a 1/2-inch-thick circle on a lightly floured surface. Cut into wedges or into rounds using a biscuit cutter. Arrange the scones 1 inch apart on an ungreased baking sheet. Whisk 2 tablespoons sugar, the heavy cream and cinnamon in a bowl until blended. Brush over the scones. Bake for 12 minutes or until light brown. Serve warm. You may substitute cake flour for the all-purpose flour for extra-tender scones.

Makes 8 to 12 scones

Carrot Bread

1 1/3 cups sugar
1 1/3 cups water
1/4 cup (1/2 stick) butter
1 cup grated carrots (about 3 large
   carrots)
1 cup raisins
2 teaspoons ground cinnamon

1 teaspoon salt
1/2 teaspoon ground allspice
1/4 teaspoon ground cloves
2 cups all-purpose flour
1 teaspoon baking soda
1 teaspoon baking powder
1 1/2 cups walnuts, chopped

Combine the sugar, water, butter, carrots, raisins, cinnamon, salt, allspice and cloves in a saucepan and mix well. Bring to a boil and boil for 5 minutes, stirring frequently. Let stand until room temperature.

Preheat the oven to 350 degrees. Combine the flour, baking soda and baking powder in a bowl and mix well. Add the flour mixture to the carrot mixture and mix until combined. Stir in the walnuts. Spoon the batter into a greased and floured 5×9-inch loaf pan and bake for 1 hour or until a wooden pick inserted in the center comes out clean. Cool in the pan for 5 minutes and remove to a wire rack to cool completely.

Makes 1 loaf

Blueberry Muffin Tops

6 tablespoons unsalted butter
1/3 cup milk
1 egg plus 1 egg yolk, lightly beaten
3/4 teaspoon vanilla extract
1 1/2 cups all-purpose flour
3/4 cup sugar

1 1/2 teaspoons baking powder
3/4 teaspoon salt
2 cups fresh blueberries
1/2 cup all-purpose flour
3 1/2 tablespoons sugar
3 tablespoons unsalted butter, chopped

Arrange the oven rack in the upper third of the oven and preheat the oven to 375 degrees. Generously butter muffin top pans. Melt 6 tablespoons butter in a small saucepan over medium-low heat. Remove from the heat and whisk in the milk, eggs and vanilla until blended. Mix 1 1/2 cups flour, 3/4 cup sugar, the baking powder and salt in a bowl. Add the milk mixture and stir just until moistened. Fold in the blueberries. Spoon evenly into the prepared muffin cups. Mix 1/2 cup flour, 3 1/2 tablespoons sugar and 3 tablespoons butter in a bowl until crumbly. Sprinkle over the tops. Bake for 18 to 20 minutes or until a wooden pick diagonally inserted in the centers comes out clean. Cool in the pans on a wire rack for 15 minutes. Remove from the cups and serve warm or at room temperature.

Makes 1 dozen muffin tops

Luscious Lemon Loaf

1 1/2 cups all-purpose flour
1 teaspoon baking powder
1/4 teaspoon salt
1 cup sugar
1/2 cup (1 stick) butter
2 eggs

1/2 cup milk
1/4 cup grated lemon zest
1/4 cup fresh lemon juice
1 cup walnuts, chopped
1 teaspoon lemon extract

Preheat the oven to 350 degrees. Grease or line a 5×8-inch loaf pan with baking parchment paper. Sift the flour, baking powder and salt together. Combine the sugar, butter and eggs in a mixing bowl. Beat using a mixer fitted with a paddle attachment until light and fluffy, scraping the bowl occasionally. Add the flour mixture alternately with the milk, mixing well after each addition. Stir in the lemon zest, lemon juice, walnuts and flavoring.

Spoon the batter into the prepared pan and bake for 55 to 60 minutes or until the loaf tests done. Cool in the pan for 5 minutes. Remove to a wire rack to cool completely.

Note: You may drizzle with a mixture of 1/4 cup confectioners' sugar, 1 teaspoon half-and-half and 1 teaspoon lemon juice.

Makes 1 loaf

Cranberry Coffee Cake

Coffee Cake
> 2 cups all-purpose flour
> 1 teaspoon baking soda
> 1 teaspoon baking powder
> 1/2 teaspoon salt
> 1/2 cup (1 stick) butter, softened
> 1 cup sugar
> 2 eggs
> 1 cup sour cream

Juice of 1/2 lemon
> 1/2 cup walnuts or pecans, chopped
> 1 (16-ounce) can whole cranberry sauce

Confectioners' Sugar Glaze
> 3/4 cup confectioners' sugar
> 2 tablespoons (about) warm water
> 2 teaspoons lemon juice

For the coffee cake, preheat the oven to 350 degrees. Mix the flour, baking soda, baking powder and salt together. Beat the butter in a bowl of a stand mixer until creamy. Add the sugar gradually, beating constantly until light and fluffy. Add the eggs one at a time, mixing well after each addition. Add the flour mixture alternately with the sour cream, mixing well after each addition. Stir in the lemon juice and 1/4 cup of the walnuts.

Spoon half the batter into a greased and floured tube pan, 9×13-inch baking pan or bundt pan. Spread with 1/2 of the cranberry sauce. Top with the remaining batter and remaining cranberry sauce. Sprinkle with the remaining 1/4 cup walnuts. Bake for 50 to 55 minutes for the tube pan or bundt pan or 35 to 40 minutes for the 9×13-inch baking pan or until the coffee cake tests done. Cool in the pan for 5 minutes and invert onto a serving platter.

For the glaze, mix the confectioners' sugar, warm water and lemon juice in a bowl until of a glaze consistency. Drizzle over the warm coffee cake. Let stand until set.

Serves 16

Easy Sticky Buns

> 1 cup walnuts or pecans, finely
>   chopped
> 1 package frozen yeast rolls (about 18)
> 1 1/2 cups (2 1/2 sticks) butter

1/2 cup packed brown sugar
> 1 (4-ounce) package butterscotch
>   pudding and pie filling mix
> 2 teaspoons ground cinnamon

Spread the walnuts over the bottom of a bundt pan sprayed with nonstick cooking spray and top with the rolls. Cook the remaining ingredients in a saucepan until blended, stirring frequently. Pour over the prepared layers. Let rise, covered with plastic wrap and a kitchen towel, for 8 to 10 hours. Preheat the oven to 350 degrees and bake for 20 to 25 minutes. Let stand for 15 minutes and invert onto a serving platter. Serve immediately.

Serves 12

Cookbook Development Committee

COOKBOOK COMMITTEE

Co-editors, Donna Jensen Roe

and Gaye G. Ingram, CCP

DESIGN COMMITTEE

Chair, Linda Cordeman

Nancy Evans

Dianne Linthicum

RECIPE COMMITTEE

Chair, Bonnie Newhoff

Linda Cathey

Leslie Christiansen

Susan Oelze

Mary Parker

Delores Tomasek

Carolyn Mendoza

NON-RECIPE TEXT

Chair, Donna Jensen Roe

Zona Lorig *(Historymakers)*

MARKETING COMMITTEE

Co-chairs, Terrie Sanford

and Ruth McLeod

Renée Donnelly

Laurie-Sue Retts

Barbara Simons

FOOD DESIGN & PHOTOGRAPHPY

Art Director, Christin Gangi

Food Stylist, Allan Schanbacher

Photographer, Werner Seggara

dinon photo

Historic Property Contributors

A special thank-you to the owners, managers and chefs of Arizona's historic properties, who worked with us to provide delicious recipes and historical information for the stories.

ARIZONA INN
Tucson
Patty Doar, Odell Baskerville

CAMELBACK INN,
A JW MARRIOTT RESORT & SPA
Paradise Valley
Terri Worthington, David Schneider, Robert Perry, Virginia Gilmore

CAMERON TRADING POST
Cameron
Mike Davis, Rudy Martinez, Josh Atkinson

THE COPPER QUEEN HOTEL
Bisbee
Tracy Glover, Chef Mike

THE COTTAGE PLACE RESTAURANT
Flagstaff
Frank Branham, Nancy Branham

EL TOVAR
Grand Canyon
Bruce Brossman, Joe Nobile

EL CHORRO LODGE
Paradise Valley
Jim Harte

FOUR PEAKS BREWING COMPANY
Tempe
Andrew Ingram, Arthur Craft, Terrence Littlejohn

GARLAND'S OAK CREEK LODGE
Oak Creek
Mary Garland, Amanda Stine

HASSAYAMPA INN
Prescott
Leonora Heintz, Peter Miller, Dusty Thurman

LA POSADA HOTEL
Winslow
Allan Affeldt

HERMOSA INN
Paradise Valley
Kelly McClellan, Michael Rusconi, Chris Cwierz

RANCHO DE LA OSA
Sasabe
Veronica C. Schultz

Recipe Contributors and Testers

Thank you to our members and friends who graciously submitted their favorite recipes and to those who opened up their kitchens for testing. Without you the tasty recipes in this book would not have been possible.

Cora Ainsa	Kay Holcombe	Bonnie Newhoff
Margaret Truman Baker	Gaye Ingram	Kay North
Kay Bates	Lynda Jenson	Susan Oelze
Linda Cathey	Sue Lennon	Mary Parker
Leslie Christiansen	Dianne Linthicum	Janice Peterson
Linda Corderman	Joan Lora	Margaret Pogue
Norma Jean Coulter	Alberta Lowry	Laurie-Sue Retts
Renèe Donnelly	Suzan Makaus	Mrs. Robey
Nancy Evans	Sharron McKinney	Terrie Sanford
Linda Fritsch	Ruth McLeod	Margaret Seeley
Susan Furlong	Noël Melin	Barbara Simons
G.G. George	Carolyn Mendoza	Pam Stevenson
Charlotte Hartman	Kari Merkow	Jeanne Stiteler
Jan Hoeschler	Jeannine Moyle	Patricia Mason Tanner
Ruth Ann Hogan	Joan Muckenthaler	Delores Tomasek
	Peggy Murphy	

Index

Mediterranean Pasta Salad with Basil, 175
Salmon Roulade, 114
Salmon Tostada, 32
Salmon with Ancho Chile Glaze, 98
Smoked Salmon Pâté, 166

Fruit. *See also* Blueberry; Cranberry; Lemon;
Orange; Pear
Stewed Dried Plums, 41

Glazes/Icings
Chocolate Icing, 137
Confectioners' Sugar Glaze, 199
Confectioners' Sugar Icing, 54
Ganache, 101
Lemon Glaze, 119

Ground Beef
Jo Jo's Black Walnut Stew, 142
Meatballs with Sweet-and-Sour
Sauce, 165
Navajo Taco, 14

Herbs. *See also* Mint; Rosemary
Basil Pesto, 89
Cilantro Lime Vinaigrette, 21
Grilled Fennel, 100
Herb Spice Rub, 44
Mediterranean Pasta Salad with Basil, 175
Tarragon Chicken Sandwiches, 149
Tarragon Tomato Sauce, 98

Lamb
Lamb Braciole, 91
Rack of Lamb with Two Sauces, 22

Lemon
Beurre Meunière, 72
Lemon Blueberry Sour Cream
Muffins, 41
Lemoncello (Liquore al Limone), 178
Lemon Rub Pie, 178
Lemon Soufflé Pancakes, 52
Luscious Lemon Loaf, 198
Very Lemon Bread, 119

Mint
English Mint Sauce, 22
Kir with Mint, 66
Minted Walnuts, 186
Mint Syrup, 26

Muffins
Blueberry Muffins La Posada, 62
Blueberry Muffin Tops, 198
Cranberry Sour Cream Muffins, 41
Lemon Blueberry Sour Cream
Muffins, 41
Muffinettes Supreme, 177
Sour Cream Muffins, 41

Orange
Chicken Salad Pie, 176
Grilled Potato Salad with Mandarin
Oranges and Rosemary, 176
Orange Shortbread, 187
Orange Vinaigrette, 120
Sour Cream and Orange Dressing, 196

Pasta. *See also* Salads, Pasta
Braised Chicken over Fettuccini, 168
Halibut with Penne and Basil Pesto, 89
Lasagna with Artichokes and
Béchamel Sauce, 161

Pear
Cranberry Conserve, 189
Mixed Greens with Pears, Roquefort and
Pecans with Celery Seed Vinaigrette, 43
Prickly Pear Barbecue Sauce, 36
Prickly Pear Vinaigrette, 97
Rhubarb Pear Chutney, 46
Spinach Salad with Warm Bacon
Dressing, 70

Pies
Apple Streusel Pie, 163
Brandy Flip Pie, 63
Chocolate Lover's Delight Pie, 152
Kahlúa Ice Cream Pie, 67
Lemon Rub Pie, 178
Margarita Pie, 124

Pies, Savory
Chicken Salad Pie, 176
Greek Spinach Pie, 194

Pork. *See also* Bacon; Sausage
Pork Chop with Chorizo Black
Bean Stuffing, 34
Roast Pork Tenderloin with Rhubarb
Pear Chutney and Pinot Demi-Glace, 44
Swiss Baked Eggs, 40

TASTES & TREASURES
A Storytelling Cookbook of Historic Arizona

Historical League, Inc.
1300 North College Avenue
Tempe, Arizona 85281
480-367-0746
www.historicalleague.com

Your Order	Quantity	Total
Tastes & Treasures at $24.95 per book		$
Postage and handling at $6.00 per book		$
	Total	$

Name

Street Address

City   State   Zip

Method of Payment: [   ] American Express   [   ] MasterCard   [   ] VISA
[   ] Check payable to Historical League, Inc., Attn: Cookbook

Account Number   Expiration Date

Telephone Number   E-mail Address

Signature

Photocopies will be accepted.